Nonprofit Boards
That Work

Given in Memory

of

Elizabeth "Bette"
Shuman

WILEY NONPROFIT LAW, FINANCE, AND MANAGEMENT SERIES

For Doug and Jessica, both my heart's desire

Nonprofit Boards
That Work

The End of One-Size-Fits-All Governance

Maureen K. Robinson

John Wiley & Sons, Inc.

New York • Chichester • Weinheim • Brisbane • Singapore • Toronto

This book is printed on acid-free paper. ∞

Copyright© 2001 by John Wiley & Sons, Inc. All rights reserved.

Published simultaneously in Canada.

This publication is designed to provide accurate and authoritative information in regard to the subject matter covered. It is sold with the understanding that the publisher is not engaged in rendering legal, accounting, or other professional services. If legal advice or other expert assistance is required the services of a competent professional person should be sought.

Library of Congress Cataloging-in-Publication Data

Robinson, Maureen K.
   Nonprofit boards that work : the end of one-size-fits-all governance /
Maureen K. Robinson
      p.   cm.—(Wiley nonprofit law, finance, and management series)
   Includes index.
   ISBN 0-471-35432-5 (cloth : alk. paper)
   1. Boards of directors.   2. Directors of corporations.   3. Nonprofit organizations—
Management.   I. Title. II. Series.
   HD2745.R586   2001
   658.4'22—dc21   00-051376

Printed in the United States of America.

10 9 8 7 6 5 4 3 2

Contents

Contents

About the Author

Maureen K. Robinson is an author and consultant on topics relating to the leadership of the nonprofit sector. Her consulting practice focuses on organizational and board development, strategic planning and executive director coaching. She is the author of *Developing the Nonprofit Board: Strategies for Educating and Motivating Board Members* and *The Chief Executive's Role in Developing the Nonprofit Board*.

Ms. Robinson founded the education program of the National Center for Nonprofit Boards and during her eight-year tenure expanded NCNB's education programs to include a national consulting service, a series of satellite broadcasts, and an annual conference that focused exclusively on governance issues.

Prior to joining the National Center for Nonprofit Boards, Ms. Robinson held a variety of positions in the museum field, including positions with the American Association of Museums and the Smithsonian Institution.

Ms. Robinson is based in Bethesda, Maryland, and can be reached by email at MKRobin500@aol.com.

Acknowledgments

I want to acknowledge with gratitude my mother's contribution to the completion of this book.

As I was tormenting the final chapters, my mother became ill, and I had to pack up my laptop and the manuscript and head to Scotland where catastrophe had befallen her. As she rested and I tried to get back on track, she would periodically call out: "Aren't you finished with that? What's taking you so long?" In all the world, probably the two questions I was least inclined to hear. Of course, she was right; it was taking too long to finish. So, I got on with it.

I also want to acknowledge and thank Martha Cooley at John Wiley & Sons who asked the same questions as my mother and almost as often, but never achieved quite the same galvanic response. I hope the book rewards her remarkable patience and support.

Most of the credit for the book goes to a handful of people who in various ways prepared me to write it. Larry Reger first brought me together with boards as we mobilized their political clout on behalf of museums. Nancy Axelrod, the founding president of the National Center for Nonprofit Boards, hired me to do the job of a lifetime and set me loose among a fair percentage of this country's nonprofit boards. Her knowledge of governance and her vision for NCNB made it an exciting place to be, both personally and professionally. Pamela Johnson has been a friend and sounding board for most of my life, and patiently allowed me to rehearse my ideas and complaints.

Finally, I want to acknowledge and thank the board members and executive directors who have invited me to work with them. My clients are my teachers. I learn something from each of them. Every day, I admire the way they approach their demanding work and feel honored to be asked to help them with some part of it.

Introduction

Over the years, I have watched many boards struggle to do a good job and I have been impressed by the good intentions and energy that a board will bring to the task. As an educator and consultant, I have experimented with various approaches to nonprofit governance, looking for a system that is flexible enough yet also precise enough to yield consistently good results for every board or almost every board. I am still searching. In the meantime, this book represents an effort to place the solution where I believe it belongs—in the board's desire to do what is best for the organization.

Boards have to shape themselves to fulfill this basic desire, and to test what they do and how they do it against the standard of the organization's best interest. There is no one way to do what's best. Boards looking for a simple formula will be disappointed. There is no perfect board size or committee structure, no foolproof way to separate governance from management. There is no universal template to guide a board meeting, no model job description that will mean enough to every board to get all 15 million or so board members to use it. I believe that people on a board know what's best for the organizations they serve better than any consultant or advisor could, but often fail to understand it or achieve it because they do not take the time to stop and consider the simple but critical question: How can we be better? The book is an effort to encourage boards to ask that question and support them when they do, to point to the areas where asking and answering the question may have the greatest power to strengthen the board's role in an organization's success.

If I could grant a board that is struggling to do a better job one wish, it would be to find the confidence and the courage to overcome the usual enemies of boardroom change—unruly and disaffected members, obsessed founders, and anxious executive directors. Where governance is concerned, money is not the root of all evil. The hours lost across the sector to people more interested in their own needs than in the needs of their organizations are a genuine heartbreak.

The nature of boards means that writing a book about nonprofit governance presents some interesting challenges. As a group, board members are not avid consumers of the literature written about them or for them. Whatever appetite they have for professional development is usually directed toward their careers, not their volunteer lives. So, the first challenge a writer on nonprofit governance must face is: Who is the reader? Who is likely to pick up this book? Will it be a board chair? A prospective board member? The chair of a nominating committee? A happy board member seeking a path to greater satisfaction? A dissatisfied board member looking for ways to make improvements?

Each of these would be a welcome reader of any book on governance. Unfortunately, the odds of a high percentage of readers falling into any of these categories, at least at first, are relatively slim. The likely reader will be an executive director, attentive as always to ways to improve perhaps the central relationship of his or her professional life: the relationship with the board.

Knowing that the reader is probably an executive director presents other challenges, particularly with the tone or "voice" of the book, and more important, with the impact of the ideas and information the book conveys. For most of the book, I tried optimistically to assume that I have the ideal reader—a board member. In one or two places, though, I break ranks and speak directly to the executive director. The bigger dilemma presented by this disjunction between the ideal reader and the actual reader is the conviction that I express throughout the book: that boards improve only because they want to, not because their executive directors or outside parties fervently wish they would.

My hope is that an executive director reading this book will feel so inspired and reassured that he or she will purchase a copy for every board member. The encouragement of the executive director combined with access to the ideas in the book will give the board what I feel is its best opportunity to become a strong and effective working body. In the event that this hope is only partially fulfilled, I have hedged my bets by focusing a chapter on the influence and the authority that the executive director does possess to leverage the board's capacity, and by emphasizing throughout the book the fundamentally positive relationship that the board must establish with the executive director if the organization is to succeed. With luck, the executive director will promptly begin to refine his or her relationship with the board and inspire the board to take on greater responsibility for its own effectiveness. In taking this approach, I am like the archer who aims high and perhaps a little wide to account for gravity and prevailing winds.

My faith in boards and my affection for people who agree to serve on them are the products of my years of working with a broad variety of nonprofit organizations, first during my tenure with the American Association of Museums and then with the National Center for Nonprofit Boards. At NCNB, I can honestly say that I worked with thousands of board members and hundreds of organizations, in every imaginable setting and under a staggering array of circumstances. A significant number of organizations made a lasting impression and their influence on this book is substantial. Many were excellent boards working deliberately to be better; others were struggling to overcome a history of bad or mediocre governance habits. A few just took off and others floundered. To me, the failures and near-misses were as instructive as the successes.

Working with boards has brought me into regular contact with others doing similar work and writing about it. Whenever I think that I have seen everything or that I have finally struggled through to a conclusion about some attribute of good governance, there is someone out ahead, by my side, or chasing after me shouting "What about this?" Periodically, I have reservations or doubts about a particular theory or approach to governance that seems to have struck a chord in the nonprofit world. Nevertheless, I am continually grateful to others working on the same topic for provoking me into thinking a little harder about what works and why, when the goal is to help improve the work of boards.

I would like to think that this book will be provoking in turn—that it will provoke some thinking, some experimentation, some change, and with luck, some disagreement. I look forward to learning about it all.

CHAPTER 1

Assigning Value:
Do Boards Matter?

I'm starting a nonprofit. Do I really need a board? (caller to a technical assistance provider)

The caller is tentative, perhaps hopeful that the answer will be no. The question itself is an interesting one—Do I really need a board? It is both a request for information and the beginning of a lament. It is a good question, worth asking: Do we really need boards?

Which is more important to a nonprofit organization, an executive director or a board? Even with the experience of watching some good boards in action, it is very tempting to choose the executive. Boards, even if they are very good at their jobs, intersect with an organization on an intermittent basis and from a distance. There may be individual board members whose relationships are more than intermittent, but their enthusiasm, as valuable as it can be, can present its own drawbacks.

On balance and given a choice, many would choose an executive director over a board. A good executive tackles the day-to-day reality of providing services, balancing budgets, motivating staff and volunteers. With the sector's pragmatism and the sense of urgency that surrounds many missions, it seems only sensible that the organization should have strong leadership where the work gets done.

This choice was not as obvious to those who established the legal framework for nonprofit organizations. Lawmakers chose the board—the first time out and every time they have had a chance to make a change. To many who work in nonprofits, it is counterintuitive that having an executive director is optional but having a board is not. Probably to his disappointment, this was the answer to the plaintive caller who opened the chapter.

While naming the board is among the first steps in the formation of a nonprofit organization, the legal requirement for a board does not really address the underlying issue of the caller's questions: What's the point of having a board? Is it of value to what I am trying to do?

Although there is substantial and often justifiable frustration with the way boards behave, the question of whether boards really matter is given only passing consideration. For the most part, we take it for granted that boards have some value, even though that value may elude us 80 percent of the time. As a practical matter, they often appear as a necessary evil, particularly to an executive director. Even an advocate of good governance and high-functioning boards, faced with a hypothetical choice and the memory of many less than stellar board performances, might be tempted to choose door number two.

The idea of alternatives to the current structure of nonprofit organizations and their governance is frequently raised but rarely burdened by examples or models that lend themselves to replication. In fact, most of the rhetoric about alternatives is more political or philosophical than practical. It is more a critique of style than of structure. The prevailing attention is focused on how to improve what is already in place—how to make it less rigid and more sympathetic to different approaches to authority and decision making—not on how to overthrow it. Despite the periodic talk of alternative structures, the recommended changes are generally superficial. Most of the attention is focused on reform rather than revolution.

Why are the immediate feelings about boards so at odds with the legal requirement to have them? Is the law perverse in this respect? Does it require people to do something that is basically useless for a reason that may have made sense in the past but does no longer? Is the form archaic? Or have we just lost track of the value of the board as we rush to get the job done on a daily basis? In our drive for efficiency, are we unreasonably annoyed at anything that appears to slow us down?

A QUESTION OF VALUE

The question of value—and linked to it, relevance—must be addressed before any serious discussion can take place about how to make boards more useful and more effective. Unless we are persuaded that boards are valuable and define that value carefully so that it meets the needs of the wide array of organizations that populate the nonprofit community, the process of making boards better is an empty exercise.

The pervasiveness of the nonprofit sector, its ubiquity, our acceptance of it, and the way it has traditionally operated make it difficult to see the sector clearly. Things may not be perfect, but they seem to work well enough. We assume the best. This complacency breaks down dramatically when there is a scandal, and lately there have been a fair number of them. A scandal certainly challenges those of us in the sector to think about how nonprofits conduct themselves; more interestingly, a scandal brings public perception of nonprofits into focus.

A scandal reveals public expectations about nonprofit conduct that under normal circumstances remain largely unarticulated. Although the average member of the general public may have only a very faint concept of what nonprofit boards and board members do on a regular basis, focus attention on an ethical lapse or a financial problem and the question immediately becomes: Where was the board? Isn't it the board's job to guard against this kind of problem? It is interesting to see how widespread this basic understanding of the board's role is within the larger culture. There may not be any clear sense of what a board's legal responsibilities are (even among many board members), but there is a widespread, almost intuitive, understanding that the board is "in charge," that it is the board's job to guard against the kinds of problems that excite investigative reporters.

At these less-than-happy moments, the value of a board becomes more understandable and transparent. At these moments, the reason why we are not given a choice about which we would rather have—a board or an executive director—becomes easier to understand. For nonprofit organizations to operate with the public's consent and with its support, someone must be understood to be acting with the public's interest firmly in mind. In this important respect, boards do seem to matter. For these purposes, boards have been assigned a value. To realize that value, they need to function in a reasonably effective way.

TRUST AND TRANSPARENCY

In an increasingly cynical culture, it is worth understanding and appreciating how much trust resides in nonprofits. Trust is what allows a typical citizen without a moment's hesitation to contribute a toy at the holidays, canned goods at Thanksgiving, and a regular payroll deduction during a workplace drive. It is what enables a neighbor to go door to door collecting for the March of Dimes or the American Cancer Society without committing the organization's most recent audit to memory or swearing to tell the truth, the whole truth and nothing but the truth, as the door opens.

This day-to-day, garden-variety trust is essential to the sector; without it we are sunk. And, just because it is easy to find doesn't make it blind. Behind that trust is the perfectly reasonable assumption that someone somewhere is keeping track of things, is assuring themselves, and by extension, the rest of us, that things are in order.

This reassurance is truly reassuring only when it comes from a person who appears to have nothing to gain from offering it. This is the reason the board, rather than any member of the staff, is invested by the public with the responsibility to keep an eye on things. When there is a scandal, we don't ask, "Where was the executive director?" (Unfortunately, in some cases, the answer is contained in the headline.) Instead, we ask the more fundamental question: "Where was the board?"

If a board had only one value—to serve as the place where the responsibility for maintaining accountability and safeguarding trust resides—it alone would justify a board's existence, and explain the requirement to put one in place right off the bat.

Certainly, that is part of what has emerged in the regions of the world currently experiencing the rapid expansion of their nonprofit, or nongovernmental, sectors. If one purpose of these burgeoning sectors is to limit the government's role in community and daily life by creating independent alternative organizations in its stead, then the sector must find ways to regulate itself that minimize the opportunity for government interference and control. There is a delicate balance to achieve between the legitimacy conferred through legal mechanisms, such as incorporation or registration with a government agency, and the freedom to pursue an independent agenda that inspires public support and trust.

Increasingly, nonprofits in other parts of the world seek a way to create "transparency" in their operations, a way to allow their motives and activities to be seen clearly and judged to be in good order. In the search to find mechanisms that achieve this laudable goal, the value of a board as an independent, voluntary, and disinterested body becomes more apparent.

REPRESENTATION AND DIVERSITY

In addition to this critical capacity to build transparency and accountability, boards offer other things of value to nonprofit organizations, things equally difficult to achieve through the agency of staff alone. One of these is the capacity to bring diversity and balance to the leadership of an organization.

Every nonprofit operates in a complicated environment, shaped by the community it serves, the mission it pursues, the sources of its support, and its relationships to other organizations allied or opposed to it. In addition, many nonprofit organizations are themselves complex operating entities with numerous gears and levers to keep in good order. In both circumstances, the board offers a way to acknowledge this complexity, to formalize and manage it, and, finally, to balance it.

As an example of this particular value, consider the national board of a membership organization. Among its functions, the board serves as a proxy for the organization's immediate stakeholders. With every election, a membership organization is attentive to the need for balanced representation at the board level—of different geographic regions, of large and small organizations, of whatever subcategories of the membership are considered critical to create a body with legitimacy in the eyes of members. Through representation, the board both accesses the breadth of perspectives it needs to make decisions in the best interest of the organization and simultaneously gains legitimacy for those decisions in the eyes of its members.

This requirement is not unique to membership organizations. Even the youngest or smallest nonprofit organization must use the board to gather to the organization the multiple perspectives that will strengthen its work and build its credibility or risk losing some of its effectiveness. No organization that attempts to address a problem or serve a particular community can ignore the value of having a board that approaches the organization's mission and its work with not only sensitivity and creativity, but also unassailable authority. Imagine the difficulty of effectively providing low-cost housing or serving the needs of young people if no one on the board can speak from immediate experience about the challenge of finding affordable housing, or of being young in today's world. The board offers a uniquely powerful mechanism to build public confidence about more than financial matters.

ADVOCACY AND RESOURCES

An additional value that boards possess—and one that, like accountability, can be achieved with greater impact by the board than by the staff—is advocacy. Most nonprofit organizations need to develop a steady stream of friends and admirers. Their missions require them to make their case and make it well. The process of persuasion is nonstop. To be a convincing advocate, one must be knowledgeable and trustworthy. Although an executive director can possess both of these qualities in abundance, the board has a unique advantage over the executive director in carrying the organization's message and expanding its circle of influence. In most of the settings in which a case must be made, the person with the least to gain by success is by default the most persuasive. The phenomenon is akin to the process of obtaining credit: only those with no need for it are likely to be quickly offered it. Because they have nothing to gain personally by their efforts, board members are powerful and persuasive advocates, a value well worth cultivating.

This power to persuade is closely allied with another value a board possesses: the power to gather resources. Boards can multiply in many ways the capacity of organizations to assemble the resources they need for their work. Although this particular value tends to obscure other values the board may possess (some of which, like accountability, are more fundamental), it remains a powerful argument in favor of having a board. Apart from the potential for raising money, the board can offer immediate and steady access to a wealth of experience and specialized knowledge through its members and through the web of relationships they can make available. Can these resources be gathered using structures or bodies other than the board? Of course. But the sense of obligation to be of service, to share knowledge and to open doors is certainly more acute among individuals who have assumed the burden of public accountability and all that it requires, than it is among a less obligated, even if no less enthusiastic, group of supporters.

CONCLUSION

In many organizations, the board is viewed in a way similar to an appendix, a part of the body without apparent purpose but capable of serious inconvenience. The combination of apparent superfluity with the capacity to inflict real discomfort makes many question the need to have a board. Seeing only their inconvenience and failing to understand their value are strong disincentives to invest in their competence and effectiveness. In this way, a board blessed with a measure of good will but little understanding of anything about its role except that it is "in charge" will fail, and in its failing perpetuate the notion that it is more trouble than it is worth.

Most boards are never given opportunities to frame a vigorous defense for their existence or to build their performance in ways that establish that they do in fact matter. Boards have the potential to bring substantial value to the work of an organization but that value will remain largely untapped if it is not understood, articulated and cultivated.

Assigning value is a necessary first step in any process designed to make boards better. We need to be convinced that boards matter before we can engage in a heartfelt effort to make them effective. Without an honest exploration of the issue of value, reforming things like composition and committee structures, or rethinking the role of board and staff become empty gestures.

CHAPTER 2

Why One Size Won't Fit All

How is it possible that in nonprofit governance, the whole is often much less than the sum of its parts? In the nonprofit community, a world well known for doing more with less and where wishing can sometimes make it so, the quality of boards can bear little relation to the quality of the people who serve on them.

This is among the most confounding aspects of nonprofit governance. Most people who join a board want to do a good job. Although a famous few will join to make mischief, it is safe to say that none deliberately sets out to do a bad job. They do not join with the intention of wasting their time or the time of their fellow board members. They do not plot between meetings on new ways to break a staff's heart or to drive the chair to distraction. And yet, innocent of these intentions, board members regularly achieve these effects.

What weird alchemy is at work?

There are one million nonprofits in the United States, and each of them has a board. They may lack staff—they may, in fact, have no staff, but each and every one has a board. If the studies are correct, the average board has 19 members.* Even

*Snapshot of America's Nonprofit Boards, National Center for Nonprofit Boards, 1997.

assuming that some people are serving on multiple boards, it is safe to estimate that at any one moment 10 to 15 million people have said yes to board service.

What have they said yes to? Most have said yes to doing what they can without possessing a clear sense of what that might be. Pressed to describe their job as a board member, a short generic list will usually emerge: to make policy (whatever that is), keep an eye on the finances, and hire and fire the executive director. This last understanding, by the way, may go to the root of the perilous state of board/staff relations in the sector. Few board members fail to grasp that at some level they are in charge. Unfortunately, being "in charge" is often interpreted as having the life and death of the executive director in their hands. To have this be the most universally understood and accepted responsibility of the board is not a comfort to an executive and often results in a range of defensive behavior that saps the life from the relationship and almost condemns it to failure.

The moment when an invitation to board service is extended and accepted can resemble a game of charades. Those who extend the invitation hint at the dimensions of the job but fail to provide a clear picture of what is required and what is expected. Those who accept the invitation guess at what is required, working with the few clues they are handed. With this as a starting point, the truth is that most board members make it up as they go along, either reproducing behavior learned in other boardrooms or, if they lack prior experience, using the first few board meetings to figure it out.

Does this make sense?

Consider the facts. Nonprofits struggle mightily to find the resources to do their work. Each of them has a board, and each board has members who at least initially set out to do their best to help the organization. In addition to their good will, they also bring, or have the potential to bring, other assets—at a minimum their time and their experience, either personal or professional. With luck and careful planning, they may also bring their network of relationships as well as their credibility and reputation in the wider world in which the organization hopes to succeed.

With all this in their favor, with such a potential asset there to be developed, why are boards so neglected? Why are they allowed to be as good as they can be or as bad they will be without more careful cultivation of this potential? In a sector hungry for resources, why are boards not viewed as the assets they have the potential to be rather than the burden or immovable object they are often perceived to be?

A part of the answer can be found in the ubiquity of nonprofit organizations in the United States, and the way most of us interact with them on a daily basis in unconscious and inadvertent ways. We might begin our day by tuning into public radio or watching *Sesame Street* with a child. We might drop that child at a day care center or nursery school, stop by the "Y" for a few laps in the pool, buzz the co-op farmers' market, spend a few hours volunteering, or head off for our day at the office. Nonprofits, after all, employ almost 7 percent of the workforce.*

In addition, in a country and a culture that emphasize independent action, the nonprofit sector is an important part of the mechanism for asserting our independence. If we see a problem and wish to solve it, or see an issue and feel compelled to express ourselves on it, we often view the creation of a nonprofit organization as a central strategy in achieving our goals. Forming a nonprofit is a way to gather like-minded individuals together, a way to organize our actions to achieve progress, a way to gain credibility, and a way to gather resources to achieve whatever one's goals might be.

Starting a nonprofit is an accessible notion to us, and the impulse to do it finds support at every turn. The local library

---

*Nonprofit Almanac: Dimensions of the Independent Sector, Jossey-Bass, 1996.

offers numerous how-to publications. The process of incorporation is not particularly onerous, and state agencies and the federal government, while requiring the usual mess of paperwork, place few real obstacles in the path to starting an organization. And finally, the nonprofit sector itself encourages growth through a wealth of technical assistance resources, from *pro bono* legal services to management support organizations.

Of course, an inevitable part of the process of forming a nonprofit is identifying those few individuals who will serve as the organization's first board. This moment may, in fact, be the critical first misstep on the road to rocky governance. Why? Because at the moment the first few board members are identified, expedience often rules our choices—"I need to list the names of people willing to serve as the organization's first directors. Can I use your name?" At that fateful moment the frequent response is not "What does that mean?" but "Sure."

THE SAME BUT DIFFERENT

Although the ease with which nonprofits and their boards are created can be a problem, particularly where the board is concerned, the result for the sector as a whole is an unparalleled diversity and richness of organizations. This diversity is as much a part of the sector's value as its independence. Among the million nonprofits we claim to have are organizations with long histories, large budgets, distinguished and important missions, and boards of stunning social and economic status. Simultaneously, we can also claim the newly organized, all-volunteer, and passionately led organizations that spring up as we (or at least a determined few people) see the need for them.

Hidden in this diversity is a wonderful paradox: nonprofit organizations have as many similarities as they have differences. They can possess similar missions and face similar legal requirements, and then diverge dramatically in terms of scale and structure. Consider an example of what this paradox means in real-life terms. Coexisting in the nonprofit community are some of the world's largest hospitals and many small but vitally important community health centers. Although at different ends of the spectrum in terms of financial resources and the size of the population that each serves, the hospital and the community-based health center are dedicated to similar and critically important missions. Each needs and deserves competent and committed leadership. Each will need to assure the people it serves that it is doing so in a way that inspires their trust, good will, and support.

With all that they might have in common, it is their differences that are most striking and that shape the ways in which they organize themselves to do their work. The differences in this example are not just about size and the complexity of programs; they also include different organizational histories, different relationships with patients and different approaches to the delivery of services.

Though each will have a board, their boards will also be very different. A visitor to a board meeting would not suffer much confusion about which of the boards was in session. One will likely have, sitting around the table, some of the community's professional and social leading lights; the other will more likely have members drawn very immediately from the community served. In one group, there is a high probability that members sit on multiple boards; in the other, an equally high probability that most are serving on a board for their first, and perhaps only, time. The working agendas for each board will be different and so will the scale of the underlying enterprises for which the boards are responsible. There might be an assumption that one board is more effective than the other because of the relative sophistication and experience of its members. In fact, in spite of the apparent advantages enjoyed by the hospital's board, it may not be as effective as it needs to be. The chances are high that some members of the hospital's board are as unclear about their role, as confused about their responsibilities, and as unable to differentiate between what they want and what is in the best interest of the organization as the members of any other board. Size and sophistication do not insure competence.

If the chair of either board were to study the most common guides to good governance in an effort to address these shortcomings, he or she would find that the recommended principles and practices they espouse ignore the basic differences between organizations and itemize a set of responsibilities to be uniformly applied to any and all nonprofit boards.

Although all boards should be effective, should they be required to act in identical ways? Are they responsible for precisely the same things? What about the notion of culture? Should the process of deliberation and decision making be the same for a large, culturally mainstream board as it is for a board that derives its members and its authority from a completely different cultural tradition?

WHAT DO WE WANT FROM A BOARD?

The example of the two organizations and their boards poses two questions. The first is how to define what the responsibilities and work of each should be given the very different circumstances in which the boards operate. The second is how to create a uniformly high level of competency within each of them.

The ability to arrive at an answer to either question requires that we back up and ask a more basic question: What do we want from boards? Other than as a useful group of people to grouse about, what is it we want them to do? Required as we are to have them, how do we make good use of them?

What is it we really want?

Well, it depends. Who is being asked this question? Is it the executive director, a donor, a board member, or the people who are served by the organization?

What does the executive director want from the board? This is certainly a very pressing question. As noted earlier, most boards grasp the concept of being in charge and see the hiring and firing of the executive director as a good example of this principle. With this reality always in the back of their minds, executive directors are highly motivated to understand what they want from their boards and to work hard to get it. This does not mean that they always succeed or even go about it in the right way. Avoidance and denial are very powerful behaviors and much easier to pull off the shelf than good sense and courage.

Catch an executive director in a reflective frame of mind and one of the first qualities he or she would list as desirable from a board would be moral support. A board needs to understand how difficult the daily experience of managing a nonprofit organization can be, and should provide the executive director with the security to act without too much second-guessing. Wisdom on the part of the board is also good and so is a willingness to work. In addition, because times are always tight, most executive directors would like their boards to be generous donors and good fund raisers. It is worth noting that although boards are often accused of micromanaging the affairs of an organization, they are rarely accused of the same level of overbearing engagement in matters related to fund raising.

Executive directors are not the only hopeful parties. Board members also have their wish lists and a vested interest in understanding what is wanted of a board. It is hard to sit through meetings and constantly wonder what the organization really wants from the board. Are we doing the right thing? Should we be doing more? Am I the right person in the right place? These are extremely important questions that too few board members get a chance to wrestle with. Instead, the doubts and concerns are expressed privately or in settings that limit their usefulness.

Although board members may bring good will to their assignment, they also look forward to some reciprocal benefits from it. They want the gratifying sensation that they have done good work, that they have had a chance to give back in some way to their communities. In the process of doing good work, they would like to experience the pleasures of good company—among their fellow board members, other volunteers, and the staff. None of this should be too much to ask. Everyone wants a chance to be smart and to have his or her talent and time respected.

If I am a client or consumer of the organization's services, what do I want the board to do? I surely want the board to be a strong advocate, to understand the bottom line and push for results. Not that I don't trust the staff, but I know that I will feel better if someone has an eye on the staff's performance and encourages them to connect what I need to what they do. If I am a donor, my list is not much different. I too want a board that assures a strong relationship between mission, program, and results, particularly for activities I support financially; given my concerns for accountability, my antennae will be carefully tuned for evidence that the board takes its ethical duties seriously.

SIMPLE versus EASY

Go back over the last few paragraphs and consider the list of qualities and behaviors that emerges through the perspectives of staff, donor, board member, and client. How difficult is it to be fair-minded or careful, generous or attentive? It must be more difficult than we think or something must make it more difficult than it should be. If not, why are the realities so often at odds with both our expectations and our not unreasonable needs?

To answer this question, it might be useful to draw a parallel. In some ways, good governance is like dieting, an area where reality is almost always at odds with expectations, not to mention needs. One of the blights of modern civilization is our obsession with weight and dieting. Out of this obsession and the willingness to spend money to satisfy it come a constant stream of books and products touting ingenious and sometimes elaborate strategies to achieve the desired results. But, truth be told, don't we all know the secret of permanent weight loss? Eat less, exercise more. Period. That's it. Granted, some engines are more fuel-efficient than others, but the principle remains the same.

Knowing how simple weight loss is does not make it easy. This is why we constantly seek new ways of doing the simple, but not easy, tasks of controlling one of life's great pleasures—eating—and increasing one of its least interesting—exercising.

Reconciling what it takes to be a good board with what most boards manage to be is very similar to the struggle to maintain an ideal weight. It may be simple but it is not easy.

There are unacknowledged complexities that shape a board's performance. One of the biggest of these is that the board, which is always referred to as though it were a unit or fixed object in the life of a nonprofit, is in fact a collection of all-too-human individuals. In addition to the characteristics, qualities, and experiences that qualified them to serve on the board, they also bring individual temperaments, attention spans, appetites for the big picture (or for the smallest detail), and habits formed in other boardrooms or the workplace. They have come on the board at different moments in the organization's development and at different times in their own lives. Whatever their intentions, their commitment and focus will fluctuate as the board's assignments change and as each grapples separately with the demands of work and family.

Other unacknowledged complexities include what each individual member assumes about his or her role on the board and the disparate motivations to be found around the table. Although good will predominates, there are other reasons that people say yes, some more useful than others. There is status to be gained by joining a board and contacts to be made. Some people want to change the world; some want only to hold the line against the passage of time. In the absence of a clear expression of what the organization requires and what the job actually entails, individual board members are free to interpret their role as they see fit, and they do.

A part of the disjunction between what an organization requires and what board members interpret as their role is the lack of a clear sense within the organization and within the board about the real value and therefore the real role of the board. The literature on governance addresses a generic organization, one with a static character and a fairly steady-state list of things to do. It does not account for the organization's stage of organizational development, its mission, or its history. It doesn't look seriously at the challenges a board faces when the board was the right match for the organization as it existed three or ten or fifteen years ago but is seriously out of kilter for the organization as it exists today. Does a group of otherwise able people have to fail in order for the mismatch between board and organization to be acknowledged and addressed?

Nor does the literature adequately address the substantial differences that can exist among boards and organizations with their roots in specific cultures, or operating within a philosophical, political, or religious context. The assumption of hierarchy embedded in the structure of most nonprofit organizations and in the structure of their boards may be intentionally overturned in some organizations. The mechanisms for making decisions—the motion, the second, the discussion, and the vote—may violate a cultural norm that values less confrontational and explicit forms of building agreement or managing disagreement.

Even if the board of a large hospital and the board of a community health center share a common uncertainty about their role and how to perform it, it is unlikely that they will be able to share a common set of ready-made solutions to address their uncertainties. As much as they may have in common, they are different organizations. How each board approaches its work must spring from a deliberate and thoughtful process of assessment and reflection, not from a list found in a book or borrowed from the organization up the street.

CONCLUSION

How do we reconcile the things that differentiate nonprofit organizations with the things that make them similar? All boards spring from a common root—the legal requirement to put one in place—but organizations quickly become wildly different and unique, placing a burden on boards to adapt. Is there a way to build a framework for effective governance that accommodates the sector's rich diversity and still feels useful and relevant to individual boards? The board of a neighborhood association may never need to recruit staff or engage in much planning beyond a balanced budget. Evaluation may never extend beyond "Great Halloween party. The kids seemed to enjoy themselves." Nevertheless, the association's board is entitled to a little guidance about financial stewardship, conflicts of interest, decently managed meetings and the wisdom of sustained leadership. The board of a national organization with a network of local affiliates will need to be prepared to do a lot more than the neighborhood association to provide effective governance, not just for itself but for the boards that link to it through its affiliates. Will both of these organizations be able to work from the same governance script? It seems unlikely. Any effort to provide uniform guidance will swamp one board and leave the other with only a gloss on its work. To be effective both boards must accept a few basic concepts that derive from their similarities, and carefully assemble the additional elements of their responsibilities that will make each board's work of value of their organizations.

CHAPTER 3

Defining the Role of the Board

For a board to be effective, the people who join it must say yes twice. The first and most common yes is to the invitation. The second and more critical yes is to the commitment to do the necessary work.

Most people find it easy to say yes to the invitation. After all, it is highly flattering to be asked to join a board. It indicates, among other things, that you have arrived, that your experience, knowledge, and standing in the community or in your profession have reached significant heights. Who could say no to an invitation with so much implied congratulation?

With an acceptance in hand, the person extending the invitation is often so relieved to hear that first yes that he or she forgets to stipulate all that acceptance entails. One of the peculiar pathologies of the nonprofit sector is the almost apologetic way in which it asks people to serve on a board. Usually, we begin with the big lie: "It won't take much time." Often, this is then compounded with an even bigger lie: "and you won't have to raise money." Is it any surprise that so many board members are guilty of not giving enough time to their responsibilities or are absent when fund-raising assignments are made?

This pattern of gross self-effacement can be tied to a number of factors, only some of which are completely understandable. Obviously, a highly attractive prospective board member will be a busy person whose time and influence are much in demand. Instead of viewing this situation as one requiring that the best and most persuasive case be made, the more common approach is to make the invitation and all that it implies as small as possible. The goal appears to be to try to slip it into a tiny crack in a person's life and hope that the obligation will be all but invisible.

What a strategy!

Which invitation is the more compelling?

I was wondering if you might be willing to come on the board. We have a couple of vacancies and were really hoping to attract someone with some financial experience. I know you're busy, but don't worry, it won't take much time. If you don't get to every meeting, we'll understand. We know you're busy. And if it's fund raising you're worried about, don't. We won't expect you to ask for money.

Or the following:

I want you to think about joining our board. It is a wonderful group of people and the organization is just fantastic. Everyone really rolls up their sleeves and it shows. We ask a lot of the board, but the organization is worth it. Everyone pulls together. As hard as it is sometimes, it is a pleasure to work together for such a good cause.

If prospective board members are genuinely busy, the last place they want to spend time is with a group that does not appear to need them. Unless the candidate's goal in life is to see his or her name on an assortment of letterheads, the invitation that will excite and challenge is to the board that is clear about what it does and needs, and is not afraid to spell it out.

For the most part (and not a minute too soon), the days of letterhead boards are past. The *quid pro quo* of lending your name to an organization on the condition that not much else will be required (or given) has been seriously undermined in the last 10 years. It turns out that the public, the press, and sometimes the law do not distinguish between those actually in the boardroom and those on the letterhead. In the public mind, if you are on the board, you are on the board. If trouble is brewing and the question is "Where was the board?" no exceptions are made. The "little understandings" that existed among some board members and the rest of the board quickly lose what little sense they ever made under the gaze of public scrutiny.

Knowing that one will be held responsible—period—has had a tonic effect on board recruitment and on the degree of seriousness with which invitations are both extended and considered. While there are still those who approach a prospective board member prepared to minimize the responsibility, the prudent candidate receives such invitations with healthy skepticism.

Now, assume that the invitation has been framed properly and the answer is yes. There is still the problem of explaining what the board actually does and why it matters. To do this task justice, it is important to place the role of the board in context and to understand how it relates to both an organization's mission and its operations. If the role of the board is not understood and defined, then it is impossible to elicit from any member of the board—new or long-term—the second, even more necessary, yes to the work itself.

THE DIMENSIONS OF THE BOARD'S ROLE

A board operates in three dimensions in the life of a nonprofit organization. It is a legal body and has responsibilities that relate to its legal duties. It is also a functional body; there is work to be done and the board is often in the best position to do it. Finally, the board is a symbolic body; a role that is critical to a board's effectiveness but is often underappreciated.

Each of the dimensions is absolutely essential to think about and to understand. They are constant factors in the life of all nonprofit boards. Although the shape and the content of each dimension will shift and alter over time, they remain a sturdy framework within which to understand, define, and adjust the board's role. To be effective, a board, whether of a soup kitchen or a college, needs to assess its role within the framework of these three dimensions, and shape its responsibilities and its approach to its work with them in mind.

THE LEGAL DIMENSION

Despite the remarkable diversity of nonprofits in this country, a common legal framework grounds the role of the board. It reflects the tradition of independence that a strong nonprofit sector both embodies and enables, as well as the practical requirement of creating within that independence a sense of public or civic responsibility that is close to self-regulating.

When a nonprofit incorporates and seeks tax-exempt status, it is required to identify a set of individuals who agree to serve as the board. They become, in effect, the stewards or guardians of the public interest claimed by the organization at its founding and for which the state is willing to confer certain benefits, including tax exemption. The establishment of a board is a minimum but universal requirement.

In the United States, each state may have different requirements about the number of initial board members, but the trend is away from a token gesture of just one person toward a still minimal but more accountable three. Those states requiring that only one person be identified discovered painfully that a single individual is challenged to provide adequate oversight of him- or herself. The temptation to self-deal or otherwise run amok lessens when there are potential witnesses.

Given the size and scope of the sector, states and the federal government have very few additional requirements to which boards must be attentive. They are silent on the subject of board size beyond stating the minimum and they do not mandate the manner in which the board organizes it work. States do usually require that boards meet at least once a year, and, like the federal government, require that nonprofits file financial information annually if their budgets exceed certain levels. Lately, the federal government has taken steps to hold boards more accountable for key organizational decisions, including the level of compensation paid to the executive director and fees paid to board members for their service. These changes and the development of what are called "intermediate sanctions" (penalties severe enough to send a message but not as severe as loss of tax-exempt status) are the result of some spectacular scandals that heightened the sense that boards must be held more directly and explicitly responsible for the actions of their organizations.

There is no escaping the fact that the board is the legally responsible body within a nonprofit organization. It is the place where the public and the state expect to find the answers to critical questions each has the right to ask. In the "deal" that allows an organization to pursue a mission of perceived benefit to the public, and that supports and encourages that purpose through special tax treatment and other benefits, the board is asked to assure that the public's interest in the organization and its work is protected.

How is this done?

In addition to the requirement that a board be formed and that it meet the rather minimal expectations outlined above, the board itself is charged with specific duties. A board has a duty of obedience, a duty of care, and a duty of loyalty. Each of the duties requires that a board and its members behave in ways that preserve the basic mission and public benefit of the organization and provide assurances that its actions support the best interest of the organization and the purpose for which it was established.

Before describing briefly what each of these duties requires in practical terms for most boards, it is important to emphasize that the board as a whole is held accountable, and that those who serve on the board are considered to be equally accountable for the board's actions. When actions are judged or evaluated, the board as a single body is held responsible, rather than individuals. While this provides individuals with important protections, it also places a responsibility on all board members to be engaged in the board's work.

It is also important to emphasize that among the three dimensions of the board's role, the legal dimension is the least susceptible to change based on things such as mission, structure, budget size, or state of organizational development. Within the legal dimension of the board's role, all nonprofits play by a similar set of rules. As organizations get larger or more complex, certain aspects of the board's legal responsibilities may be delegated to others to fulfill, but they are never wholly relinquished by the board. The board may elect a treasurer and the organization may hire a bookkeeper or chief financial officer but neither action permits the board to divest itself of its legal responsibility to provide financial stewardship. In the same way, an executive committee, even if an effective mechanism for structuring the board's work, does not relieve the full board of its fundamental legal obligations.

DUTY OF OBEDIENCE

An organization is granted tax-exempt status because its mission and purpose are considered to be of public benefit or because it meets other requirements that entitle the organization to preferred status as a corporation. A board is charged with the duty of obedience to assure the state and the public that the organization continues to operate for the purpose for which it was formed, that it is *obedient* to that purpose, and that the organization operates in compliance (or obedience) with the laws that govern and regulate it.

The board must monitor an organization's actions for consistency with the organization's mission. It must also monitor other forms of legal and regulatory compliance. Is the organization required to file annual reports with state and federal governments? Are its operations, including its personnel functions, in compliance with government requirements? Are its employees expected to have and maintain certain credentials and licenses to continue to provide services?

The nonprofit sector may not be heavily regulated, but there are people and places paying attention. For example, the board of a relatively small community-based organization discovered a few years ago that payroll taxes were in arrears only when the state rather aggressively pointed it out. While board members were surprised to learn the executive director had solved a cash-flow problem by finessing the payroll taxes, they were shocked to learn the government was prepared to hold each of them personally accountable for the amount due.

DUTY OF CARE

Luckily, boards do not always need to be right. They do, however, need to demonstrate that they have been careful. What constitutes *careful*?

It is in meeting the duty of care that the habits of a board are formulated. To demonstrate care, it is important that a board meet with regularity, that meetings be well attended, and that the discussions and decisions that take place at these meetings be well informed, candid, and documented so that others can judge how careful the board really was.

In this area, boards and board members are encouraged to be guided by the "prudent person" standard, which requires that actions be judged by whether a prudent person given the same information and the same circumstances would have reached the same decision.

Clearly, every board needs to determine for itself how often it meets and the content of its agenda. Many things will influence this, including whether an organization is local or national in focus, how large the staff is, whether the organization is in crisis or highly stable, and whether it is just beginning or has a long history that sustains it. All these things may influence the decision about how often to meet, how to communicate, and what issues to focus on, but the final determinant is the needs of the organization for good oversight and effective leadership. Boards need to test their work habits to assure they meet their obligations to their organizations and to the public for accountability. The duty of care should bring out the best in a board; it should make it attentive, prepared and fully engaged.

DUTY OF LOYALTY

Of the legal duties required of a board, the duty of loyalty is simultaneously the easiest to understand and the hardest to judge. Most people understand the need for all decisions to be reached with the best interests of the organization firmly in mind and predominating. It is unacceptable to make decisions that have as the primary beneficiaries individual members of the board, their business associates, or their friends and family. But opportunities for missteps or misperceptions are common—the accountant on the board who provides accounting services, the lawyer who provides legal advice, the banker who facilitates a line of credit.

Everyone's antennae are up when a decision appears to involve a conflict of interest between the board, or a member of the board, and the organization. Those reservoirs of trust and confidence on which nonprofits depend are easily jeopardized if a board has failed to act in a manner free of conflicts of interest. Even the perception of conflicts of interest can create a crisis of confidence. A newly formed nonprofit might initially include members of the founder's family and close associates and excite no concern. But as the organization matured, became more stable and attracted broader financial support, the tight-knit composition of the board would invite skepticism: How objective can the board be? Will the obligations the board members have to each other and the founder outweigh their obligation to the best interests of the organization? Even if the answer to both questions is no, the widely perceived potential for conflicts of interest will undermine public and donor confidence in the organization.

In every organization, the opportunities for conflicts of interest will differ, and the steps a board takes to avoid having its actions second-guessed or misunderstood will also differ. What remains constant is the obligation to consider what the most likely opportunities for potential conflict will be and to agree on how these should be acknowledged and avoided. The duty of loyalty places the burden directly on the board to be vigilant in maintaining an organization's integrity and its focus on the public's benefit.

THE FUNCTIONAL DIMENSION

In addition to being a legal body, the board is also an important resource for getting the job done.

In a startup organization, the board may find itself the chief cook and bottle washer. Without a staff, an organization may rely heavily on the board to perform critical staff functions, including program and service delivery, bookkeeping, public relations, and fund raising. In a very mature organization with a large and professional staff, the board will spend its time differently. It may not actually balance the books, but it has just as great an obligation to assure that the books balance. Relieved of one particular task, board members may have numerous others that budget size and organizational complexity require them to undertake on a regular basis. They may need to master the detail of public policy as a prelude to active lobbying rather than answer phones, or they may need to study and evaluate the best approaches to investing endowment funds rather than take a direct role in the delivery of services.

No board is exempt from being useful. Whatever the organization, there is work to be done. The nature of the board's work and the balance between board and staff will shift as time, talent, and circumstances require. Executive directors who struggle to find things for the board to "do" are usually suffering from an acute failure of imagination or from insecurities too deep to allow them to treat the board as a resource for taking care of the organization's business.

This takes us back to the issue of understanding that board members must say yes to the *work*, not just to the invitation to serve. It is critical to define what the work is in order to animate people's participation and to give the work meaning. The functional dimension of board service is often reduced to a tidy list of responsibilities: support the mission, hire the executive director, evaluate the director's performance, understand the financial performance of the organization, assist with fund raising, and so on. While all of these tasks may constitute part of the board's work, lists are not animating documents.

Having been handed a list of responsibilities, a board member is not likely to be effective because the list has been read, or even agreed to. A board's function—its work—must connect in obvious ways with the needs of the organization. For instance, as the board undertakes the significant task of recruiting a new director, do I, as a board member, understand why it is important for us to hire the best person for the job? Have we thought hard about what it is the executive director needs to be able to do for the organization over the next three to five years? Have we really looked carefully at candidates? Now that we have someone on board, have we been thoughtful and candid about our expectations? Are we united in articulating our goals? Are we ready to work with the executive director to achieve them?

Each of the common assumptions about board responsibilities must be reexamined to determine whether the board needs to do more or less of it, needs to do it differently, or needs different people to do it. The previous chapter made a case for why boards have value. This value is not abstract; it is not about public perception. It is about putting the board to work in ways and on issues that have value—measurable value—for the organization.

THE SYMBOLIC DIMENSION

The board is a leadership body. The process of identifying and recruiting the people who serve on the board is a way to capture concretely a broad array of attributes that the leadership body must encompass to be effective and to be credible. These include skills or experiences with practical value as well as characteristics that communicate a complex message about the organization's status, its values, and its claims for credibility.

37

Who serves on a board conveys an important message to clients, constituents, members, donors, and the community at large. An international organization has to identify strong leaders from around the world, not just from one country or hemisphere. A new organization must attract at least a few well-known and well-respected leaders to stake its claim to serious attention from its community and donors. One national medical organization advocating for the health needs of women realized that while its board had many women on it, none was a doctor. All of the doctors on the board were men. Given its health-related mission and the status of doctors in that field, failing to include a woman with a doctor's professional status created a symbolic dissonance that was evident to both policy makers and the organization's constituents. Another organization wanted its board composition to send a clear signal about the multidisciplinary nature of its work and provided equal board representation of certain fields even though those fields were not proportionately represented among the membership. The organization was willing to risk an accusation of disproportionate representation of some fields to preserve the more important symbolism of its multidisciplinary nature.

Despite the earlier warnings about letterhead boards, the list of board members and their identifiers—gender, nationality, race, ethnicity, profession, community status, prestige—tells a story about what the organization values and therefore wants to possess in its leadership body. This is not about tokenism or the empty gestures of the letterhead; this is a legitimate dimension of the board's role and should be considered as carefully as other dimensions are. In addition, the powerful symbolism of the board is not a story that is constructed once and then handed down from generation to generation. It is important to update the tale and to reinvigorate it. The ability of the board to function effectively in this dimension, like any other, requires regular reassessment and redefinition.

ANIMATING THE WORK OF THE BOARD

To be effective and to be of genuine value, boards need a way to connect what they do with what the organization needs from them. Board members need to see the results of their involvement and participation, not just find themselves at the end of a meeting with the agenda fully covered. This may sound obvious, but think about how often this vital connection lapses or fails to materialize. Consider the number of boards that can barely pull together a quorum for a meeting. These boards have failed in fundamental ways to connect the board's work with the work of the organization. Or, consider the boards with dwindling numbers of members that are unable to think of anyone to recruit to join them. They have lost so much confidence in what they are doing they can't even extend the invitation to serve, much less outline the nature of the board's work. It is rarer than it should be to serve on a board and see the difference or appreciate the contributions you have made to the organization's success.

How to begin to change this? Once again, it is simple but not easy. It requires time and a willingness to explore the meaning of serving on the board, rather than taking that meaning for granted. It requires the intellectual and emotional commitment to insist on a fully engaging and fully engaged board experience and an unwillingness to settle for less.

Consider carefully the role of the board within its dimensions as a legal, functional and symbolic body. How well and how closely has the board defined what the organization needs and what the board does so that the board has both meaning and value? Is the board an integral part of the organization or a ceremonial body that engages in empty ritual?

If the answers are not in place, it is time to develop them. To begin to redefine and to reanimate the purpose and the effectiveness of the board requires that very basic questions be asked and answered honestly:

- What is the mission of the organization? Does everyone agree on it, understand it, support it? Is it a mission that moves us individually and collectively to do our best?

- What needs to be done? Are some tasks essential for our future? Do we understand what matters?

- How can we accomplish the work? What will it take? What do we already possess as an organization? What are we lacking?

- What can the board do? Is there an assignment that only the board can do, or that it can do best? Is there a way to be of genuine assistance to the staff?

- Is the board prepared to do its work? What don't we know? What do we need to learn? Who is missing? Whom do we need to bring onto the board to get the job done?

- Are we ready to work? Is everyone committed? Are we ready to say goodbye to those who aren't ready, willing, or able?

- Can we pause for a little reflection in six months or so to see how we are doing, congratulate ourselves for doing better, and fine-tune the parts that aren't working?

Equipped with answers to these questions, a board is ready to begin meaningful work on behalf of the organization it has agreed to serve—not a theoretical organization or a typical organization, but the specific organization it must serve and help to succeed.

CHAPTER 4

Boards That Work: The Structure of the Work

To echo an earlier refrain, the theory of governance is relatively simple. It's the practice that is difficult.

The difficulty of performing well as a board is easy to under-estimate. People, particularly executive directors, hope that by reading and absorbing the theory of good governance a board will begin to perform in a manner that resembles a world-class orchestra—all members in place, their parts understood, finely tuned, note-perfect. Once everyone has assembled, all that will be needed is the director to produce the score and the chairman to tap the baton lightly to begin.

Even when a board has grasped its essential purpose and thought carefully about its responsibilities, the concepts that sit so securely on the page often rest only lightly on the mind. It is easy, for example, for a board to know that an important part of its job is to hire a good executive director, evaluate his or her performance, and change leadership if the executive director is not effective. It is a little more complicated actually to do those tasks.

What can get in the way?

Finding and hiring the right person can be hard. Evaluation? Let's face it, who wants to be the one to deliver bad news about performance? And firing? Firing is even more complicated. What if the executive director is the founder? It takes a lot of energy, not to mention confidence, for a board to replace the founder. What if the founder chairs the board? How does the board resolve the conflict when the founder/chair has difficulty relinquishing any part of his or her authority to the executive director and undermines the director's performance at every turn? What good is a firm grasp of theory to a board faced with these complications?

To be fair, personnel issues are always difficult. A better example might be the theory that the board is responsible for fund raising. A significant part of the economy for fund raising and board consulting would collapse if boards took the message of fund raising to heart. Imagine a world in which just learning about the importance of fund raising immediately prompted board members to ask friends, family, and strangers for money. The board's role in fund raising is a message that can be repeated endlessly, appear to be understood ... and then promptly be put to one side. By its actions, a board seems to say: We know we should, we feel bad we don't, but we just can't. It's too hard!

A board that works must work at two levels. First, there must be an inherent logic in the board's existence, a certain inevitability to it. The board has to have internalized the reason it exists and its value to the legitimacy and success of the organization. It needs to add to the sum of organizational energy rather than exhaust its members and the organization's staff by flailing regarding in confusion about its role.

In addition, the board that works must also work in the humblest sense of the word. It needs to contribute in practical ways to getting the organization's job done. Why have a board filled with talented and experienced individuals and not use those assets to help the organization get from point A to B? It would be like having the world's best clock and not using it to learn the correct time.

Good boards, boards that work, do not spring forth fully formed from the head of Zeus. They rarely change overnight and they rarely change because of a book or consultant, no matter how persuasive. Unfortunately, they also rarely change because the executive director wants them to. Boards change because *they* want to. They change because they believe that the mission of the organization and all of the people involved in realizing that mission deserve to have as good a board as possible. The catalyst can come from anywhere, but without an agreement in place among the members of the board that the time has come to be a good or better board, theory alone will not do it. Theory without the will to put it to practice is like rain against a window; it beads and clings but finally slides away.

To get good at governance takes practice.

The orchestra members do not show up the evening of a performance, however handsome their clothes or fine their instruments, and give a good performance without training and a little bit of practice. Unfortunately for boards, there are few places to learn good governance. An aspiring executive director can find a wealth of opportunities to learn new skills, and can take a few years working at lower levels in nonprofit organizations to practice the skills needed to be an effective director. A board and its members do not have the same opportunities. In most cases, the board, like an orchestra, is already on the stage and in the middle of a performance when members are asked to take a seat in the string section. Under these circumstances, we can hardly expect great music, despite all the good will in the world.

As boards focus on improving their performance, it is important to acknowledge one of the fundamental challenges of building an effective board—the board's inherent and irreducible complexity. A board is not a fixed, uniform entity. It is in a fairly perpetual state of flux and transition. People join the board and leave the board. They attend some board meetings and not others. Some members have a gift for the big picture and others need the anchor of detail to feel confident about what is going on. Some remember every slight or disagreement; others cannot recall what happened at the last meeting.

There is no simple way to create a board that works in every sense of the word. The key is to seize as many opportunities as possible to give the board a chance to understand its job and practice it. This chapter looks at the most common and accessible activities for doing this. The next chapter looks at powerful but more complicated intersections between the board and the content of its work. The purpose of each chapter is to make use of the most commonly available opportunities a board has in the normal course of its existence to work hard, better, and more effectively on behalf of the organization it serves.

MEETINGS

One of the opportunities most available to any board for improving its performance is the board meeting. The board meeting is without doubt one of the most reviled aspects of board service—yet where else but at a meeting is the board fully itself? Certainly committees, task forces, and other similar groups keep the wheels oiled and often produce good results, but they do not substitute for the power and authority of the board when it meets as a body. A board is just a theory, just names on the page, until it comes together in a meeting in as close to its entirety as possible to do the organization's business—to work.

Board members are right to revile meetings. Most are terrible, and not much is done to make them better. It is amazing how bad they are. We suffer through them with an unusual degree of fatalism given the basic optimism of the nonprofit sector. There seems to be an assumption that organizing and running a good meeting is part of the cycle of human development and will come as naturally to a mature adult as walking upright. On the evidence, this assumption is deeply flawed and needs to be revisited.

Meetings matter. Board meetings are the starting point and the foundation for a good board and effective governance. The meeting is the place at which theory can most obviously and most easily be converted to practice. A study of board practice by the National Center for Nonprofit Boards indicates that boards average nine meetings a year, so there is ample opportunity for improvement.*

THE RULES OF ENGAGEMENT

The discussion in this chapter focuses on the content of meetings and not on their form. There are a number of extremely good resources on the mechanics of conducting a good meeting and these should be on the reading list of every incoming board and committee chair. Most organizations find that some version of the formulations found in *Roberts' Rules of Order* helps to make meetings manageable. Even if they are only Bob's Rules, a consistent and fair set of rules help to set the boundaries for discussion, encourage order and civility, and clarify decision making.

An important caveat about the potential misuse of rules of procedure should be stated: The rules are there to serve the larger needs of the organization by helping the board to arrive at good decisions. They are not there to trap unwary board members into conceding to decisions against their will or better judgment because of procedural missteps.

*A Snapshot of America's Nonprofit Boards, National Center for Nonprofit Boards, 1997

Certain procedural questions from board members almost always signal trouble. They typically concern bylaws and *Roberts' Rules of Order*. In fact, these questions rarely are about the technical issues that are raised; more often, they are an attempt to use rules to circumvent or trump an opponent. No one really cares about the bylaws unless a fight can be won or a question quashed on the basis of a close reading of an obscure section, subsection, paragraph, and line. Similarly, the rules question is not about a fluctuating quorum and a tabled amendment and a clutch of proxies; it's about winning the issue on points. Boards cannot do good business in such narrow and mean-spirited ways. Somewhere between chaos and tyranny is a way of conducting a meeting that presents the real issues fairly, allows for thoughtful and respectful discussion (even disagreement), and yields decisions that further the best interests of the organization and the people it serves.

TRAPS FOR THE UNWARY

Once a procedural form for discussion and decision making has been refined to bring out the best in everyone, the board can turn its attention to the serious issue of content. There are two important things to remember. First, boards work on what is in front of them—no issue too great, no issue too small. At a minimum, the agenda for a board meeting should be evaluated to be certain that the items requiring decisions really belong to the board and not to the staff, particularly not to the executive director.

The second thing to keep in mind is that boards do not have a natural braking mechanism that allows them to stop and study the way they habitually do things. It is rare for a board to say "Let's stop meeting so often or for so long," or "Let's meet longer next time to give an issue the consideration it deserves." It is equally rare for a board to say "How do we hear from everyone and not just the same three people?" or, more problematic, "How do we avoid hearing the same things stated over and over again?" Most boards tend to replicate their behavior—good and bad—from meeting to meeting without entertaining the possibility that things can be improved. Even when board members privately wish for change or stand in the parking lot complaining bitterly to each other, the individual desire for change is not commonly translated into a collective will for improvement.

THE EMPTY VESSEL

Meetings also suffer from the empty vessel theory. In this theory, the board meets a fixed number of times a year, for a traditionally fixed period of time. Whoever has the responsibility for framing the initial agenda approaches each meeting with those two things firmly in mind. The question then becomes: What are we going to do at this meeting for two (or whatever) hours? Let's see, approval of the minutes. The executive director's report. The financial report. All right, where are we for time? Hmmm, those three things will take about 40 or 45 minutes tops. Okay, what else . . . what else? What will we do for the next hour or so?

Under the empty vessel theory, the meeting *must* take place if this is the first Thursday of the month and that is when the board has always met, and the agenda must expand to fill the regularly allotted time . . . *no matter what*.

Combine the empty vessel theory with the two earlier observations—the willingness to work on anything and a helpless inability to cry "stop"—and it becomes clearer why board meetings can undermine the genuine desire of board members to do a good job. There can be a whole lot of nothing going on.

HOW GOOD MEETINGS GO BAD

Although stories abound to illustrate this phenomenon, the following tale seems sadly on point. The pastor of a church housed in a historic structure came to the lay board with the need to replace the church roof. Because of the complexity of replacing the roof, the pastor had already researched the handful of contractors who could do the work. At the meeting with the board, the pastor outlined how she would propose to solicit proposals, set out what she thought the approximate expense would likely be, and suggested that a small committee work with her to evaluate the proposals. The board quickly approved this strategy. A month later, the pastor and the committee returned with a recommendation which the board, after a brief but cogent discussion, accepted.

At the same meeting, the pastor mentioned the need to lock the church's office doors during business hours for safety reasons. She planned to have some kind of doorbell installed and was thinking about a door release system to make it easy to buzz visitors in. After having spent less than 30 minutes on a major capital expense, board members began an exhaustive discussion about the doorbell: Should it chime or buzz? The local hardware store had a good selection. There was probably a parishioner who could help install it. What about the release mechanism? Didn't that require some kind of speaker system to work, or maybe a camera? Who did that kind of work? To the chagrin of the pastor and a number of board members, this discussion threatened to continue in perpetuity. In the blink of an eye, the board had gone from high functioning to low.

When meetings go wrong, there is usually more than enough blame to go around. The temptation to run amok is very strong and the original culprit quickly draws others into the fray. The roof came to the board in a carefully structured set of proposed steps and recommended actions; the doorbell landed on the table innocent of any thought. Although few members of the church board knew much about putting a roof on a historic building, they all knew something about doorbells. It only took a moment for doorbells to go from housekeeping to governance.

MAKING MEETINGS WORK

The burden of making meetings work falls equally to the board chair and the executive director. The pastor should have resisted the temptation to fill airtime with a routine matter, and the chair should have closed down the discussion as quickly and as gracefully as possible. Although executive directors may feel victimized at moments like this, the executive director has more power than is generally acknowledged to shape the issues that come before the board in order to bring out the best in the group and to avoid placing inappropriate matters on the table. Equally important, the board chair has to play an active part in determining both the agenda and the conduct of the meeting. Neither party is doing his or her job if agendas are primarily designed to fit the time available and the discussions and decision making that result are flabby or, worse, counterproductive.

Although it is very important to ask if the items on an agenda relate to governance or management, determining which is which can be consuming and contentious. It is more useful to ask whether an item or issue is important to the organization and deserves the board's attention or needs board guidance or approval.

The Test of Importance

Boards need to spend the bulk of their time on things that meet the test of importance. Certainly, there are routine matters that require the board's attention and approval, but these can usually be dealt with clearly and quickly. It should not take long to understand and make a good decision with respect to the signatures on a bank account, or to establish the policies that will govern the parameters for day-to-day financial transactions. These kinds of matters relate to the board's responsibility for accountability and oversight and cannot be neglected. Nevertheless, it is possible to frame and present decisions of this nature in ways that honor the board's responsibilities without consuming unreasonable amounts of its time.

The challenge for the executive director and the board chair is to evaluate which matters rise to the definition of *important*. To do this, there are a few useful guides:

- Does an issue touch meaningfully on the values of the organization? As we think about, discuss, and act on an issue, are we faced with concerns about a principle of importance to us, or a value that is integral to our sense of who and what we are as an organization?
- What about public opinion and perception? Is the board going to be happy living with a management decision if it has to defend that decision in a public arena?

Even if an issue can safely be placed in the management column, the staff may need to extend the discussion to the board. Not all decisions involve values and principles, but those that do tend to transcend the normal parsing of responsibility between the board and staff and warrant the board's involvement. The same is true of decisions that will be closely scrutinized by the public, stakeholders, or even staff. It is more important for an organization to be able to speak with one voice than to maintain management's right to a decision.

The Test of Scale

Another useful test involves scale. Is an issue genuinely a big deal? Does it have significant financial or personnel ramifications? Is management comfortable with assuming full responsibility for the decision? This is a particularly tricky area because the penalties are stiff for misjudging the issue of scale. There are executive directors who would like to have as little responsibility as possible and will use the board as a convenient escape mechanism, and there are board members who have never met a decision they didn't think they should have made, particularly if a decision made by management is revealed as flawed in some way. In these circumstances, second-guessing qualifies as an Olympic event, with board members sweeping all the medal categories.

The Test of Consequences

The last test for building the board's agenda is the conjunction of planning and evaluation. Even organizations that do not have strong strategic plans have goals and expectations about performance. The mission demands that the organization accomplish some part of its purpose, and the board's responsibilities demand that some accounting take place to measure whether the mission is being met and whether resources are being used wisely. In many respects, this is what a budget is—not just a mess of numbers, but a concrete expression of what will be done in the span of a year and how much it will require in human and financial resources.

As the executive director and the chair consider the issues that should come before the board, they should be able to sort through a potential agenda for the items that deal with goals and the accomplishment of mission. If such items appear to be missing more often than not, it may be time to start framing them for the board's agenda. If one of the board's key values is to provide a mechanism for maintaining public trust, it must develop the habit of asking good questions about both expectations and results. For this to become a healthy habit, opportunities to do this must be presented to the board on a regular basis and structured in a way that helps the board to do it well.

WHAT ARE WE DOING?

With a good agenda, an executive director and chair have a solid platform on which to build the meeting. Before they call the meeting to order, however, they can take a few other steps that will help the board to work to its capacity. The first of these is a quick determination of what action each agenda item requires of the board: is it a decision, are we seeking advice, or are we exchanging information that helps to keep everyone up to date as an issue develops or matures?

In the absence of direction on these matters, the board is likely to default to decision making. Decisions are how boards express their sense of authority. For a board without a clear sense of its role, random decision making can be the autopilot of governance. The executive director who fails to appreciate this fully takes some terrible risks. It is hard to know which is more painful: watching a board struggle to make a decision with only a dab of information in front of it, or witnessing the panic of the executive director who is about to be saddled with a decision when all he or she wanted was a little advice. Presenting an agenda with the actions required of the board clearly labeled is a simple step that yields big rewards in helping a board to do good work.

HELP FOR THE DECISION-AVERSE

Having painted a dark picture of the consequences of unrestrained decision making, it is important to note the problems that can occur at the opposite extreme. The power of the board meeting to build board performance depends not only on the avoidance of bad decision making but also on the careful orchestration of inescapably necessary decision making. Even if not all the items that come before the board require a decision, those that *do* require a decision . . . require a decision! Boards cannot avoid the responsibility of making decisions and hope to be effective or to be of value. They have to choose a course, saying yes to some things and no to others. They have to provide enough clarity to enable the staff to move ahead with confidence and authority.

Some decisions are tough; few are foolproof. It is possible to meet the standard of care, exercise diligence, be an extremely prudent person, and still be wrong. It is hard for a board to risk being wrong, particularly when the consequences may be borne by others. It is in fact so hard that delaying or avoiding decisions can seem like a safer bet. Boards do not have that luxury if they want to do a good job.

It falls to the chair of the board to facilitate and support good decision making. On behalf of the board, the chair needs to determine with staff that the information at the heart of a good decision is available and that the elements of the decision are presented clearly. If there are options, they need to be described; if there are consequences, they need to be stated; if there is a recommendation, it needs to be supported.

By assuring the board that it has the information it needs, the chair can task the board to make a decision and then help the board do this well by managing the decision-making process. At this moment, the chair is both a facilitator and a disciplinarian. A board needs room for constructive discussion and debate. Honorable people can disagree. The only rule for disagreements among board members is that in taking differing positions, all parties be motivated solely by the best interests of the organization. The chair makes sure that the rule is followed and that a healthy discussion takes place.

The chair also helps to keep the discussion on track and to bring it to a close. An argument can be stated only so many times before it loses its power to sway. Having said that, all arguments should be aired. Withholding an opinion during the course of a board discussion is as detrimental to a good decision as repeating the same one over and over. What is the opinion being saved for? The postmortem in the parking lot or the phone call the following day? Neither place is as helpful to the organization as sharing an opinion during the course of the meeting itself.

The chair needs to help the board review where the discussion stands, test to see that the discussion has been complete, and identify whether a consensus is emerging. If the chair feels that the board has all the information it needs and has had adequate time to discuss an issue, he or she has to resist unproductive requests for additional information, limit repetitive discussion, and call the question.

SEIZE THE OPPORTUNITY

Bringing this level of attention and planning to a meeting may appear to be overkill, and it may in fact be a burden to the board chair and the executive director if the board is meeting more than it should or if the staff is unused to pulling supporting information together in advance of agenda planning. Nevertheless, it is a mistake to treat meetings as anything other than the central moment in the life of the board and the key to its effectiveness and real value. No other board activity provides such a consistent context or a similar variety of potential issues and tasks. If one is in search of ways to develop the board and improve the practice of governance, the board's meetings offer some of the richest opportunities.

COMMITTEES AND OTHER ASSIGNMENTS

As important as the board meeting is for building the capacity of the full board to do good work, there are other mechanisms available to advance that goal. One is the effective use of committees and other subsets of the full board. There are few boards that do not begin to subdivide into committees almost at inception. The formation (and reformation) of board committees appears to be an honorable effort to distribute the work of governance more equitably among members and make use of board members' expertise or their appetite for specific areas of the board or organization's work.

Committees, task forces, and advisory groups are all potentially powerful ways to boost both board and organizational productivity. A board committee can provide a level of engagement with an aspect of the board's larger responsibilities or with a specific issue that is difficult to maintain with the full board. The finance committee is a good example of this. The full board does not relinquish its responsibilities for the planning and oversight of an organization's financial well-being by creating a finance committee. Rather, by creating the committee, the board is calling on a few highly engaged and knowledgeable board members to monitor financial issues in greater detail and in greater depth on the board's behalf. The committee enables financial monitoring to occur between board meetings and makes it possible for complex aspects of financial performance to be properly understood and presented to the board in a cogent manner. In addition to being of service to the board, the committee may also represent a substantial asset to the organization and its staff, providing advice, expertise, and a place to "rehearse" financial issues before they go before the full board.

A Tool for Leadership Development

In addition to their value in streamlining certain board tasks, committees are also a tool for leadership development. Although the board is a leadership body, the body itself needs leadership and needs mechanisms for developing and sustaining it. Committees can provide a set of platforms within the board on which various members can demonstrate their commitment to the work and their capacity for leadership. Chairing a committee, or just serving as a visibly capable member of one, allows individual board members to demonstrate to their peers their diligence and good judgment. This helps to build the confidence and trust that a leader will need from the board to be effective.

Make Them Meaningful

When committees work, they are hard to beat, but they are not good in and of themselves. Subdividing the board and assigning each committee a name are not enough. Naming a chair and assigning people to serve on committees are not enough. Committee structures, particularly standing committees of the board, are too often treated as articles of faith—a part of the belief system called good governance. They are sometimes itemized and described at great length in the bylaws. In fact, we have such faith in committees that a job description for individual board members will often require service on at least one of them.

If meetings serve as empty vessels, committee structures often serve as sponges, sopping up members to fulfill the job description, or to complete the board's table of organization: if the board comprises 20 members, and each member has to serve on at least 1 committee and a good committee size is 4 or 5, the board will have to have at least 4 or 5 committees, not counting the executive committee. Voilà! Typically, these will be a finance committee, a program committee, a development committee, and the nominating committee, or some variation on similar themes. Ambitious boards or those with more members may have additional standing committees, either to sponge up members or to leave no aspect of the organization unsupported or overlooked by a committee. Under these circumstances, chances are high that the quality of committee leadership will be uneven and that not all committees will have enough to do. After a few years of this formulation, the board chair and the executive director will spend as much time trying to jump-start the committee structure as they do preparing for meetings or engaging in planning.

Returning to the assumption that board members are in fact eager and willing to do a good job and bring some heart to the task, the disappointment is disproportionately acute when the initial enthusiasm for serving on the board is met by activities, such board meetings and committee assignments, that seem beside the point. Listless, ineffective committees can infect and detract from an entire board's performance. How long will a board member believe that his or her participation on the board is of value if meetings don't matter and committee assignments are an empty gesture?

COMMITTEES FROM SCRATCH

The key to building a committee structure that works and that enhances the board's overall productivity and sense of accomplishment is a willingness to start from scratch each year with every committee. Get over the muscle memory of the traditional committee structure. Stop believing that every single board member should serve on a committee. Let committee leadership rise or fall on whether a committee gets its job done and all of its members had a chance to participate.

Finally, it doesn't matter what the group is called. Committee, task force, ad hoc, standing, advisory—spending time distinguishing one from the other and creating some kind of hierarchy may be one of the reasons the committee structure is moribund.

57

A Committee's Purpose

Begin to build a functional committee structure by asking why the committee should exist and what it will do. If the full board needs to think through its role and shape its agenda to be of value to the organization, a committee has to do at least as much.

The process of inquiry does not begin by asking, for instance, what the program committee needs to do this year. Instead, the question is more basic: What significant governance responsibilities involving programs must be addressed this year? Define the committee's charge by beginning with what the board needs from the committee rather than what the committee needs to do to perpetuate itself or to be useful to the staff. This could involve updating plans and objectives for programs and recalculating resource requirements. It could involve rethinking or restating program priorities, or assessing the impact of changes in a client population or the funding environment. It might be time to evaluate how effective a program strategy has turned out to be.

It could be one of those things, two of those things, or none of those things, but the committee is not formed until it is clear that it has a purpose—a *charge*. In a given year, there may be a number of major program-related tasks that have to be handled either simultaneously or over the course of time. Perhaps rather than one program committee, it makes more sense to have a number of smaller, more carefully focused committees working on governance-related program matters. The structure should support the needs of the board and of the organization, not merely produce a tidy organizational chart.

This is one of the virtues of regularly starting committees from scratch. The board has greater flexibility to get the job done and avoids having one committee working around the clock while another sighs and twiddles its thumbs. It also allows the board chair some discretion about assignments that arise during the course of normal board business. With flexi-bility rather than structure, and results rather than form as the dominant characteristics driving the creation and use of com-mittees, matters that require deeper study or thought do not automatically get referred to an existing committee, but can be handled in more pragmatic and immediate ways.

Tasks and Time

A committee needs a plan of work and a timetable both to keep itself on track and to enable its work to be useful to the board and the organization. For the nominating committee, this is obvious; the committee has to produce a slate of candidates by the time of the board elections. Other committees are not blessed with as clear an imperative to get their jobs done. A reasonable deadline is a useful thing, particularly for busy people. It makes it easier to see what tasks have to be per-formed and in what order, and builds accountability. It also streamlines the delegation of assignments to allow a number of people to take responsibility for getting the work done (not just one do-it-all type).

Committee Leadership and Membership

Once the purpose is clear, it is easier to know who will have the talent and expertise to lead the charge (so to speak). The chair of the board must make the match with task, talent, and time in mind. In addition, the matching process should occur annually. Only by appointing people for a year or until the assignment is completed (whichever occurs first) does the chair liberate committees from the tyranny of lifelong appoint-ments. In addition to assuring that committee leadership is kept fresh, the one-year appointment also creates a healthy velocity for leadership development purposes.

The balance of the committee's membership should also be carefully considered. Depending on the charge and the required tasks, the committee may need to incorporate a certain breadth of perspective or a politically potent cross-section of personalities. It could also as easily require a very small membership with a laser-like focus on getting the job done.

I am biased in favor of the smallest committee consistent with getting the job done. There is a strong argument from my perspective for creating committees of two, as extreme as that might sound. Two people will always find each other. The third person is almost always missing—and it is never the same third person. This means that a large part of the committee's time will be spent trying to get the third person on the line or at the meeting and a good part of the balance of the meeting will be sent bringing the person who was missing from the last meeting or conversation up to speed.

Committees and similar groups (task forces, advisory bodies) also provide a board with at least the opportunity to consider involving non-board members in the work. This flexibility is particularly useful if the board is small or if the committee's charge will be more successfully accomplished if the committee has included a breadth of perspectives not wholly found on the board.

ADVISORY BODIES AND HONORARY BOARDS

Sometimes the governing board is not enough. Occasionally there are special topics or special tasks that require going outside the competency to be found on the board or among the staff. Forming advisory bodies is a way to capture, on an ad hoc basis, the expertise or perspective that the organization requires without adding talent to the board to meet every contingency. When used for this purpose, an advisory board is a valuable solution to what is usually a temporary need.

Like a board committee, an advisory body needs a clear charge and a plan of work. It also needs additional clarity about its status in the organization and its relationship to policy making. Unlike a committee of the board, an advisory committee has no consistent frame of reference for identifying its role in the organization. It may be linked to the governing body or it may be linked directly to the organization through the staff. To do a good job, it needs to know what, if any, authority it has. People may be gratified to be asked to give advice, but the gratification lessens if the advice they give is ignored or put to one side. In the absence of direction, an advisory group, like a governing body, will assume as much authority as it can, forcing the board and staff to react to it. Any ambiguity about its role has the potential to create dissatisfaction and possibly conflict.

Many advisory bodies come into existence to resolve a problem or head one off before it gathers momentum. If this is a genuine motive behind their creation, they can be an invaluable resource. In contrast, an advisory committee is rarely effective purely as a delaying tactic or a way to co-opt potential critics; whatever time is gained will be lost when the tactic fails, which it eventually will. A museum's experience with a version of this tactic is a good illustration of its shortcomings. The museum appointed a community advisory group to react to its education and outreach activities. This was partly in response to the staff's desire for a well-informed focus group and partly to forestall grumbling about the lack of community representation at the board level. The members of the advisory group were at first happy to be involved, but after a year of meeting with staff and providing feedback on various programs, they felt as though they were spinning their wheels. They were not consulted when programs were in the planning stages and were left making suggestions that would have been costly and inconvenient to accommodate (a situation the staff recognized and wanted to change). It was also apparent to the committee's members that no one on the advisory committee was any closer to being invited to serve on the board than they had been a year earlier. Instead of a resource, the committee quickly became a point of contention. The education staff was left to reformulate a more effective version of the committee under a cloud of suspicion, and the board found itself looking distinctly small-minded when its motives were cast as exclusionary.

Honorary groups present different opportunities and different potential problems. The most common types of honorary groups are created to capture the support and the credibility of well-recognized, powerful figures who cannot easily serve as board members, but are willing to confer their name—and with it their imprimatur and implicit approval—on an organization or one of its activities. It is a useful strategy if everyone understands that these individuals are not members of the governing board. The public association of certain political figures, celebrities, or well-known professionals with a particular organization has powerful symbolic value that is most often useful for advocacy or fund-raising purposes. There may have been a time when high-profile people who could lend their names but not pledge their time or attention were included on the board, but increasing levels of public scrutiny and concerns with liability have for the most part put an end to this practice. The creation of honorary groups, if done correctly, is an alternative strategy that achieves a useful purpose.

A less successful kind of honorary category is the one created to serve as a repository for retired board members and founders. It is less successful than the version of honorary bodies just described for a number of reasons. Although it is important to honor those who have made substantial contributions to the creation or the success of an organization, gratitude may not need to be expressed as a permanent relationship with the organization's governance. To soften the blow of retirement, honorary members of the board are often allowed to retain certain privileges, such as attending board meetings. This means that people with no legal responsibilities and technically no accountability have the same access to discussions and deliberations as members of the governing body. If all distinguished retired board members were wise, this might not be a problem, but this is not a guarantee. There is also the problem of managing organizational change in front of people who feel an attachment to and partial ownership of the past. Finally, if there are no term limits for honorary members of the board, there is the unappealing prospect of former board members having longer access than any of their successors to opportunities for shaping strategy and influencing policy.

Creating a classification for honorary board members requires careful thought. If it is just a way to postpone the moment to say "thank you and goodbye," the board chair and the nominating committee need to take a deep breath and do their job to maintain the integrity of the board and the quality of its members. If it is a genuine desire to honor a founder or extremely valuable board member, it is better to create a limited number of emeritus positions with full board responsibilities than to create a category with an unlimited number of untenured members and an ambiguous relationship to governance.

CONCLUSION

Boards meet; they subdivide to get complicated issues ready for discussion; they prepare; they discuss, disagree, and decide. All of these activities are not only natural to a board but also essential if it is to govern the organization and work on its behalf. These activities can be pursued in a heedless, catch-as-catch-can way that reflects long-standing habits or the idiosyncrasies of a handful of people, or they can be pursued deliberately with an eye to making the most of their value to the practice of good governance. There are times when careful scrutiny and recalibration of the forms of board practice can lead to improvements in the board's function and the substance of its work. It is always easier to work in a clean, well-lighted space than in a cluttered hallway with a buzzing fluorescent fixture. Too many boards work in the equivalent of the cluttered hallway. It is an unnecessary hardship and a grave distraction. A more carefully organized agenda, more useful background materials, and more functional committees require an effort to achieve but not a revolution. The ease with which these changes can be made argues strongly for beginning the process of strengthening the board at its next meeting by asking simply how the meeting could be better.

CHAPTER 5

Boards That Work: The Substance of the Work

Part of the challenge of developing a board that works is addressing simultaneously both the mechanisms that make efficient, useful work possible, such as meetings and committees, and the substance that makes work meaningful. One cannot be sacrificed to the other. A board grappling with big, consequential issues squanders its energy and loses its focus if the work is poorly organized. A good infrastructure—meetings that are productive and committees that understand their assignments and complete them—makes the most of people's efforts and avoids duplication and delays. By the same token, a board that is highly organized but empty of content benefits no one. Its value to the enterprise is questionable and the commitment of those who serve on it will evaporate. Meaning trumps efficiency, even when very busy people are involved.

A handful of issues comprise the content of the board's work. They are few but potent. This chapter considers three of them: financial oversight, planning and its adjunct task evaluation, and, finally, fund raising. In many respects, these are the bread and butter of board work. While bringing a mission to life or articulating organizational values may have large and overarching importance for the board and for the organization, a typical board will spend substantially more of its time on an organization's finances, its plan, and the need to develop resources than anything else. These are the heart and soul of the legal duty of care. To be a competent board—a board that works—these tasks must be done consistently and well. The complexity of each of activity may vary, but in their essentials, they transcend issues of size and organizational maturity and belong to every organization, whether wholly volunteer or supported by staff.

A bias will be evident in this chapter. Financial accountability, often seen as a mechanical or technical part of a board's work, is given pride of place. This has been done very deliberately. Many more nonprofits struggle and fail because boards neglected to be attentive to the way resources are allocated and used than fail because their formal planning processes are deficient. The burden of financial failure falls hardest on the people the organization is supposed to serve. Board members usually get to move on from these failures and very little onus attaches to them, but the youth center that closes or the community clinic that goes bankrupt deprives people of access to important services, and deprives employees of a livelihood.

In emphasizing the board's responsibility to be a competent financial steward, no disrespect is meant to the value of planning or the need for boards to engage in fund raising. But both of these processes, in their complexity and in the almost cult status they have achieved in the nonprofit sector, will be quickly eclipsed if the board is not attentive to the underlying financial health of the organization.

Planning and fund raising have a glamour attached to them that financial accountability will never acquire. The written resources and technical assistance available to help a board pursue them effectively are impressive and accessible.

Unfortunately, the opposite is true where financial stewardship is concerned. In training courses and workshops, I learned never to schedule the topic after lunch; it was difficult to ignore the nodding heads and not a little demoralizing. It is tough to make the subject attractive, much less glamorous, so this chapter settles for urgent. This chapter strikes an unambiguous blow for the board's obligation to be minimally competent about financial matters, and in a positive but less insistent way encourages boards to plan, evaluate, and raise money.

FINANCIAL OVERSIGHT AND ENLIGHTENED CURIOSITY

The best talent a board possesses for providing strong oversight is its natural curiosity. Unlike the staff, which witnesses the life of the organization on a daily, moment-to-moment basis, the board intersects with an organization much less frequently and in highly ritualized settings, such as board meetings. Suffering from a form of sensory deprivation, it is natural for board members to wonder about what is going on and equally natural for them to want into the loop: What has happened since the last time we met? What's the good news? What's the bad news? How did that project turn out? Did we get the grant? Is the budget balanced?

In fact, viewed from this perspective, the agenda for a board meeting is, in part, an organized effort to respond to a board's natural curiosity and make that curiosity productive. Any effort to satisfy the board's appetite for news should succeed in converting idle curiosity into enlightened curiosity, thereby harnessing what might be an annoying impulse into one that serves the best interests of the organization. Ideally, we want to create and sustain a healthy attention span, one that appreciates complexity and feels rewarded for both asking good questions and receiving thoughtful responses.

In financial matters, this means providing useful information and presenting it in formats that invite the best kinds of questions, ones that make it possible to learn something useful on behalf of the organization.

This goal is easily thwarted. The greatest obstacle to a board's oversight of an organization's financial well-being is the aversion within the larger culture to anything that looks like arithmetic. We are a nation of math phobes. If proof of this is needed, one need look no further than America's nonprofit boardrooms. While people may speak blithely of the bottom line or lament the effect the lack of one has on nonprofit accountability, the truth is that most of us couldn't put our finger on the bottom line if our very lives depended on it.

It is hard to read a nonprofit balance sheet and almost as hard to make sense of a fairly straightforward statement of income and expenses. The language itself is counterintuitive. How can a commonly understood benefit, such as a foundation grant, be characterized as a liability? How can members' dues, sitting so plumply in the statement of cash flows, look so ominous on the balance sheet? What is depreciation really? And, by the way, where is the money we spent to replace the computers?

Aggravating the lack of basic navigational skills among board members when faced with pages of financial data is the increasing complexity of nonprofit accounting. We have cost-centered accounting, we have restricted and unrestricted funds, we have a new category of virtual income—multiyear pledges that may or may not materialize but must be treated positively in the year in which they are made, but then get discounted or adjusted to reflect the likelihood that some people will fail to fulfill their pledges . . . I think. Even board members who have a grasp of financial matters have usually mastered them in the business world, and can be as baffled as any novice by the technicalities of a nonprofit's financial reports.

To illustrate this state of affairs, imagine the board meeting of a very successful nonprofit housing corporation on the morning the audit is presented. The board of the housing corporation is a wonderful mix of people. There are bankers and clergy, there are real estate developers and construction experts, there are people knowledgeable about community planning and there are people who are consumers of low-cost and affordable housing. This board is blessed with a carefully nurtured spirit of collaboration, buttressed by a record of accomplishment. The orientation and ongoing education process are designed to make everyone as smart and knowledgeable about the affairs of the organization as possible. The executive director and the board have worked hard to make the most of each board member's expertise and point of view as well as to minimize, particularly for the consumers on the board, any differences in educational attainment and income levels that might hinder the full and equal participation of every board member.

The accounting firm has sent a representative to present and discuss the audit. He is serious, thorough, perhaps a little lugubrious. (In my experience, not many accountants are poets; it is probably a handicap for an accountant to have too much imagination, or sudden flights of fancy.) When he has finished his presentation, he asks for questions. A relatively new board member raises her hand. She is a "consumer" member, but feels no diffidence about her lack of an accounting background. Her question is this: She understood that the housing corporation had a surplus in the last fiscal year, but as she looks at the first page of the audit, she doesn't see the surplus anywhere. What happened?

As she asks this question, it is apparent that many on the board, not just her fellow consumer representatives, consider it a good question: "That's right. We had a surplus. Where is it?" They lean forward in their seats ready for the answer. And the answer presented by the auditor is this: "You are looking at the balance sheet; it balances." In case she missed his meaning or didn't feel foolish enough for asking, he added: "That's what a balance sheet does: it balances." Oh. Of course. It balances. Now everything is clear.

As the woman struggles to deal with her embarrassment, a high percentage of board members are breathing a real sigh of relief that she asked the question before they did and spared them this public humiliation. Even as the moment passes, the event has more serious consequences for the board. The woman has decided never to come back, and the rest of the board has learned how risky it is to ask questions about financial statements.

At the conclusion of this drama, a quote of George Bernard Shaw's comes to mind: "All professions are conspiracies against the laity."

Although the conspiracy we suspect exists where nonprofit accounting is concerned can appear to be particularly diabolical, board members must acknowledge the extent to which they are co-conspirators. There is a strong temptation; to which many board members succumb, to remain ignorant and to leave the math to others. Without a good faith effort to resist temptation, it is impossible for a board to fulfill one of its central responsibilities: to see that resources are well used and carefully accounted for.

Ignorance doesn't always begin and end with the board. Executive directors, particularly in smaller nonprofit organizations, often lack the depth of management experience that would provide them with strong financial skills. Budgeting can be unrealistic or simplistic, and reporting can be inadequate. This is noted not to excuse a board's less-than–stellar performance as a financial steward, but to point out that, in most cases, the board can only be as good as the executive director and bookkeeping staff will allow it to be. It is a good illustration of the way board capacity is linked to staff capacity. This book cannot remedy problems with the staff's capacity. Nevertheless, it is a serious handicap for a board to lack the rudimentary tools it needs to perform its work.

Instead of lamenting this state of affairs, let's assume that the board has what it needs (or is close to having what it needs) to do its work. The challenge is to find techniques for getting that work done and done well.

NO STUPID QUESTIONS

For a board and staff wrestling with the best way to increase the financial stewardship of the board, the first step is to agree that in principle there are no stupid questions. Asking questions is the only way to learn something. Though the result is not always guaranteed, as the earlier story illustrated, not asking questions makes it a virtual certainty that you will remain in the dark.

A corollary to the "there are no stupid questions" principle is the general rule that if one person doesn't see it or get it or understand it, the chances are high that he or she is not alone in this confused state. For this reason, questions should also be viewed as a kindness extended by one board member to others.

The best questions a board can ask are the most basic:

- Are we ahead or behind?
- Is our spending in line with our budget?
- What accounts for the differences?
- Are we on track for the rest of the year?
- Is there anything we should be concerned about?

A slightly more complicated set of questions is also pretty basic:

- What is the most important source of revenue for the organization?
- Is it rising or falling as a percentage of our operating budget?
- What is the fastest growing expense that we have?

- Are we working to control it or have we got a plan to cover it?
- Does the budget support our goals for the organization?
- Are we spending money where it matters the most?

THE ANNUAL BUDGET PROCESS

Although these questions usually emerge after the budget has been presented and approved, it would be a mistake to overlook the budget development process and its important and fundamental role in the board's stewardship of the organization.

Often, perhaps too often, budget preparation resembles the making of sausage: It is sometimes better not to know what goes into it. By experiencing only the final product and ignoring the unsavory and unattractive parts that serve as its raw material, we protect our innocence and make enjoyment possible.

In a similar way, budgets are also consumed in a manner that leaves the board with its innocence delicately intact. The numbers, and the process used to arrive at them, emerge shrouded in mystery. Did the organization take the previous year's budget, correct for obvious errors, factor in inflation, and hit the total key; or did it deconstruct its programs and activities and reassemble them to arrive at the budget that was presented? Did the organization's plan play a part in the allocation of resources, or did that worthy document do a disappearing act? Did the organization estimate its expenses and then project an income to match, or do the income figures represent a separate effort to gauge what could realistically be expected to materialize in the course of the year?

In a good example of the triumph of optimism over experience, a museum board approved successive budgets that balanced only because the estimated results from a special event were pegged at a level that made the balancing act possible. The fact that the event had never generated anywhere near the level of net revenue projected for it did not influence the decision to include it in the budget every year. The new executive director, who had been carefully charged with eliminating the deficit, not only did not maintain the fiction in the first budget she presented, she argued for eliminating the event entirely because it had failed to achieve any perceivable goal. The board fought tooth and nail both to keep the event and to estimate its income at its previous upbeat level. This year, the board promised, it would hustle to sell tickets and promote the event. After sizing up her chances of changing the outcome of the discussion, the director made other adjustments in the budget to cushion the effect of the likely shortfall, vowing to live to fight another day.

The museum director experienced first-hand what can happen when a board moves from the role of critic to that of creator during the development of the budget. The development of the budget belongs to the staff. Unless the organization is volunteer-driven and the board is for all intents and purposes the staff, the board does not have the kind of knowledge of organizational life required to assemble a good budget. The board *does* have the capacity and also the obligation to be an informed and diligent consumer, and therefore a critic, of the process as well as the product. A good treasurer will be able to ask and answer the questions posed earlier about how the budget figures were calculated and certify the budget development process to the board, but the board continues to have the responsibility to review the budget, understand its implications, and ask questions about it. It cannot avert its gaze from the sometimes unsettling reality that must guide the budget process, nor can it insist that the staff garnish the results to make them more palatable.

As this critical framework for organizational life is developed, it is important to remember that a budget is a snapshot, not a moving picture. It represents only a single interval in an organization's life, even if that interval is complex. Presented by itself or only in reference to the preceding year's results, it allows such a brief and narrow glimpse into the organization's story that little sense can be made of what is revealed. It's like trying to imagine a face when only a foot is visible. By comparing the proposed budget for the coming year only with the experience of the year about to end, the typical budget presentation cannot yield the level of insight a board needs to do its work. With these two sets of numbers as a guide, can a board determine which changes from one year to the next constitute a trend, and which are short-term phenomena?

Is a budget in balance the only thing that should matter? On the surface, it is certainly better than a budget that doesn't. But this is where the board's role in understanding the meaning and implications of the budget as both a process and a product can be critical. The simple truth is that a budget that carefully balances, and does so year after year, may conceal a calamity in the making. There is more to running a meaningful nonprofit organization than getting the books to balance. Important programs and services can be contracting year after year after year, because the staff and the board have failed to find the resources to keep them at a healthy level. The organization may have kept itself out of immediate financial danger, but it has taken the graver risk of becoming completely irrelevant.

It is not easy to move from producing financial snapshots to creating financial moving pictures, but it is an area where a board can add value. By pushing for as broad a view of the organization's financial life as possible, rather than the glimpse offered by the budget document, the board avoids accepting a perspective that has only momentary value. By insisting on numbers that reflect reality, the board averts the magical thinking that makes financial crises inevitable. By asking that the budget mirror the larger goals the board and staff hope to achieve for the organization, the board challenges itself to help make them happen.

The key to these happy results is an acceptance that, to an honest board, the budget is not the place to preserve one's innocence or play the innocent bystander. In some cases, it may be the only plan an organization has the resources to produce and, therefore, needs to be taken seriously. Even when a more comprehensive plan is in place, the budget deserves a board's full attention; it is the tool within easiest reach as a means both of making any plan happen and of evaluating results.

GOOD FINANCIAL INFORMATION

Moving from the moment when the budget is approved and returning to the board's enlightened curiosity, the next set of intersections between the board and the financial performance of an organization will be the monthly or quarterly reports that materialize (or should) at each board meeting. The ability of the board to ask good questions at these moments presumes that a certain amount of raw material is in place to support a decent level of inquiry.

Financial statements and reports are a good illustration of the difference between data, information, and knowledge. Data are facts. They may be important, but their importance doesn't make them useful. Only a context succeeds in making them useful and moves them closer to the preferred state of providing information. A board definitely needs information— information is its working capital; but, even with a wealth of information, a board needs knowledge more.

Knowledge implies some discernment; it represents a judgment that some information is more useful and has more meaning than other information. Knowledge allows for insight and, with luck, wisdom. It is conveyed only by a process of carefully connecting the dots—selecting the data and providing a context—in a way that tells a story. As the story presents itself, it is possible to draw conclusions, and if not conclusions, at least a clutch of very good questions.

Good financial statements and reports tell a story about the organization's performance. They allow actual performance to be measured against expectations and they allow comparisons to be made to similar periods of time. They allow board members at a glance to see the financial facts of an organization's life. Good financial statements and reports contain only essential information and they present this information clearly and concisely. Board members can enter the process of reading these documents as amateurs and still do a credible job of understanding the basic story being told. With good raw material, they can exercise enlightened curiosity and ask good questions.

This is the most basic level at which all board members should be able to operate in their role as financial stewards. There is no reason for a board member to relinquish his or her responsibility for good financial oversight to an executive director, the board treasurer, or a finance committee. Although more complex analyses may be assigned to others on behalf of the full board, the basic grasp of an organization's financial life must be within reach of all board members if the board is to do its work and meet the duty of care.

PUTTING A FOUNDATION IN PLACE

This blessed state is not achieved through wishful thinking. For the most part, it is achieved through a combination of teaching and taking responsibility.

Any formal orientation program for new board members should include an introduction to the financial life of the organization. It should not only cover how to read the organization's financial statements but also provide a detailed look at the significant underlying facts of the organization's financial life: the major sources of support, the challenges inherent in generating revenue, the major categories of expenditure, how these relate to the strategic plan of the organization and the priorities implied in it, the way the budget is developed, the process of approval, the mechanisms for staff accountability.

In addition, the orientation should include a little historical background that highlights either the stability of the organization's financial life, or the nature and scale of changes that are influencing current financial performance. A community-based youth organization had what could be viewed as a very healthy budget, one that was in balance and appeared to reflect a dynamic realization of the mission. However, it was not clear to the board that the budget had doubled at one point in the recent past and had experienced substantial increases for a few years after that.

What looked like a healthy and hard-charging organization was in fact a very fragile place struggling to accommodate its growth, and the demands of that growth on its staff and organizational infrastructure. Some of the new money was very difficult to manage; it was restricted, required sophisticated bookkeeping to account for properly, and, more ominously, was available only as reimbursement for work and activities as they were completed. This last aspect of the new money generated serious cash-flow problems for the organization.

Most of the board members had little feel for this history. Those who had been on board for awhile were pleased at the growth; those who were new had no basis for forming an opinion. The recurring and increasingly serious cash-flow problems finally forced the board to pay attention and begin a painful process of accumulating more knowledge. The problems with cash flow and the board's weak grasp of fiscal realities ended up compromising the relationship between the board and the executive director. From viewing the director as a gifted visionary and capable manager, the board began to question the director's most routine actions and reports, demanding more and more assurances that nothing—no little bit of information—had been left out.

The executive director in this example might be faulted for providing a less-than-thorough orientation, but he cannot be blamed for the board's failure to take responsibility for its own performance. The board routinely depended on the executive director to reassure it about financial matters and demanded little in the way of reports. Financial statements were often distributed at the meeting, rather than being sent in advance, and there was rarely time available during meetings for board members to read over reports and formulate questions except those of the most obvious nature. Even the treasurer was often seeing reports for the first time at the meetings and depended on the executive director to provide an overview on the spot. Questions that couldn't be answered at the meeting fell between the cracks. Apologies were offered at every meeting for the failure to get reports to board members in advance, but "the organization was growing so fast and everyone was working at such a hectic pace that time just ran out."

In this example, the board conspired with itself and the director to avoid reality. There was no withholding auditor who deflated well-intentioned efforts to learn. When all was said and done, the board ended up with full responsibility for the jeopardy into which the organization was tossed, as well as for the reductions in programs for the young people it served.

TREASURERS AND FINANCE COMMITTEES

In spite of the board's ultimate responsibility for financial oversight, not all of the heavy lifting is done by the full board.

Most boards have a treasurer and most have some version of a finance committee.

The treasurer of the board is a classic good news/bad news phenomenon. The good news is that a conscientious treasurer can bring a level of attention to an organization's financial life that it would be both unrealistic and inefficient for the full board to attempt. A good treasurer can increase the rate at which information becomes knowledge for the board by performing an important editorial function, screening a wealth of events and transactions to uncover and highlight the telling few. The treasurer can perform a much closer analysis of significant financial information than most board members are prepared to keep track of personally. Together, the treasurer and the staff can take a systematic look at a variety of important financial trends in the organization over a longer period of time and distill the information that will be shared with the board.

The treasurer, on behalf of the board, can look below the numbers to see whether they reveal efficiencies or deficiencies. Does it matter that an organization now spends more on certain client services even as the number of people it serves has declined? A typical financial statement does not reveal this information, and most boards would waste considerable time—theirs and the staff's—in trying to learn it on their own. This makes it a perfect assignment for the treasurer, who can pull this information together quite quickly with the staff and in doing so enable the board to ask good questions about why this has happened and what, if anything, it means.

The bad news about treasurers is the extent to which a board will quickly and with the greatest relief relinquish its responsibilities to this officer. Feeling grateful to be freed of the task, the board often fails to hold the treasurer to any decent standard of performance, thus avoiding the need to find some other willing victim for the assignment. After the role of board chair, treasurer is the most dreaded and assiduously avoided job on the board. So unpopular is the assignment that board members willing to take it will sometimes end up holding the position for long periods of time. This can result in a loss of rigor and in an idiosyncratic, personality-driven perspective of the organization's financial performance. A long-tenured treasurer compounds the challenge of accountability for the board. The potential for loss of face if problems arise that should have been noticed earlier creates a disincentive to reveal them that is all too human.

There are a number of things that argue for having a finance committee. First, the committee is a good place to develop "bench" talent for the treasurer's position, a definite plus. It can also spread the responsibility of closely monitoring the organization's financial affairs among a group of equally competent but differently talented individuals. One may have an appetite for carefully scrutinizing costs, another may bring professional accounting experience to bear, another may understand how investment policies are established and the results evaluated, yet another may provide a larger focus that spots trends and can relate them to environmental changes. This multiplicity of talents represents an alluring ideal and one well worth pursuing.

Even with the ideal in place, the finance committee needs periodic scrutiny to be of value. The risks it presents are twofold. The first is the problem that all committees present: Does the committee work in deed as well thought? The second is the temptation, always out there, for board members to run from this particular job, leaving it for others to do.

Run, perhaps, but definitely not hide. Boards have a legal duty to demonstrate care and the additional obligation to be accountable to donors and constituents. In the area of financial accountability, there is an alternating current between what the organization and the staff must do to support the board's responsibility and the responsibility of both individual board members and the board as a whole to meet this standard and fulfill these obligations. As difficult as it might be to master the basics of building a budget and reading financial statements, as hard as it might be to become a demanding consumer of well-presented and intelligently constructed reports, these are essential parts of a board's work, parts that must work well if the board is to succeed in bringing value to the organization and the people it serves.

PLANNING AND EVALUATION

Although the annual budget may be as much of a plan as some organizations ever manage to put in place, it is not a document that takes an organization very far. While nonprofits often feel their existence is fragile, few can be satisfied by a plan that only takes them forward a month at a time, and makes no guarantees beyond a year. This flat-footed approach to the future goes against the inherent optimism that is an essential requirement for working inside a nonprofit. After all, in a certain light, most missions could be seen as organized efforts to tilt at windmills.

Even the most cautious board resembles a group of early explorers. Early explorers had difficulty believing that the horizon was not the edge of the earth. The borders of their maps hinted at the horrors that lay beyond. Nevertheless, despite their fears, what lay beyond enticed their imaginations. A board committed to its work but with little to guide it will find itself experiencing much the same trepidation mixed with curiosity about the unknown. For a while, the board will work with the map it has, whatever its shortcomings, and be glad that the edge never materializes, but over time it will become more than a little curious about what is just beyond the horizon.

This appetite to look ahead is one part longing and one part common sense. We are willing to be visionaries, but not dreamers. We accept that progress requires movement, that decisions will need to be made about each step along the way if what we imagine and long for is to be achieved.

At a minimum, a good plan provides a context for decision making. At its best, a good plan marries vision and ambition to a rigorous pragmatism. It enables an organization to make the most of its mission. It contains a fair—not inflated and not self-punishing—assessment of the organization's strengths and weaknesses; it acknowledges, rather than ignores, an environment in which there are limits but also possibilities; and, finally, it contains mechanisms to judge whether the plan is working.

Although developing a plan is not a destination in and of itself, getting there in good order helps to ensure the success of the rest of the journey. The literature of nonprofit governance and management is rich in instruction and guide books for the planning process. If these seem inadequate, the literature in the business sector offers additional theories and methodologies, some of which adapt nicely to organizations without conventional bottom-line measurements of success.

The challenge may not be too few resources but rather too many. Planning has spawned some very elaborate, almost religious, systems, and a priestly cast of authors and consultants. It has become a little like the ads that warn don't try this at home! Although a little outside assistance can help to build a productive planning process, going it alone should not be made to feel as risky or as naïve as standing in a bathtub with an electrical appliance in one hand and the plug in the other.

Even the vocabulary of planning has competing advocates, and many give the most common words such nuanced meanings that they become opaque and difficult to use clearly without appropriate body language or special fonts. Long-range planning has given way to *strategic* planning—such a better-sounding word. Very careful distinctions are made between *goals* and *objectives* when the dictionary is happy to treat the two words as synonymous. In planning, we don't just research what is happening outside the organization that is worth understanding, or assess how the rest of the world perceives us: we conduct *environmental scans*.

Is it any wonder that boards struggle with the planning process and often lose their way?

Both the process and the product of planning have to be a good fit for the organization and the board. Keep it simple, keep it useful. Before embarking, gauge the organization's (particularly the board's) appetite for process, the amount of time available, the money in the budget for an outside facilitator, and the urgency with which a plan must be devised. Choose a process that balances these factors, and begin.

The board's role in planning and the board's use of a plan are not identical to the staff's, and the reasons to plan will also differ. Attention spans are widely variable, and this variability must be acknowledged. Plans generally cover a five-year period, but it is useful to test whether the board, the staff, or the organization (given the operating environment) can maintain its interest in a plan for five years, will lose track of it after two or three, or will find that the plan lacks staying power and is quickly overtaken by events.

There are many great-looking, great-sounding, and sometimes very expensive plans quietly gathering dust on a shelf behind the executive director's desk. Some plans never develop a constituency in the organization; others never create the momentum to influence decision making. A plan will fall flat if there is a lack of faith in the process or a lack of confidence in the future implied in the plan. If the organization has consistently failed to meet its fund-raising goals, a glorious future that depends on every board member becoming a powerhouse asker and giver is going to engender either deep skepticism or deep depression as the most basic results fail to materialize.

Some plans are doomed for more complicated reasons involving the temperament and personality of an organization's leaders. Leaders can make or break the planning process and their personalities are often insuperable obstacles to any plan other than the budget. A strong-willed director who reflexively resists any "interference" with her vision will find the planning process gravely inconvenient. The board chair who rejects the notion that an organization can manage its future to any significant degree or who views planning as a variation on navel-gazing is going to prove an impossible person to engage. There is unfortunately little good advice to offer in these circumstances. Planning is not an alternative to therapy, although hope does spring eternal in the minds of those trapped in working relationships with such inflexible and self-absorbed personalities.

Intractable personalities aside, it is important for an organization to acknowledge whatever challenges the planning process will face and create a process that minimizes deficits and makes the most of assets and opportunities. A formal planning process must be more than a bow to the conventional wisdom that planning is good, and more than a wholesale reproduction of the current best-selling approach to the topic. Each organization needs to adapt and improvise—to make the process work for the organization and, just as important to make it work for the board.

Good plans are leadership documents as well as powerful management tools. This point was brought home by the board of an association of healthcare educators during their most recent cycle of planning. They approached the planning retreat with a carefully pulled together document outlining the results of months of staff work, committee work, and member surveys. It was a fair representation of the thoughts and opinions that had been gathered during that period and was a good first draft of a plan. In the preceding four years, the association had used its existing plan to good effect, which helped set the tone for the retreat. It had been a document that board and staff found useful in their different capacities. As the plan unfolded from year to year, it had proven a good indicator of performance and a flexible tool for allocating the association's staff time and resources. Most important, it had enabled the association to make the most of its opportunities.

The completeness of the draft document and the experience with the existing plan created a perfect platform for the planning retreat, but the moment felt thin. The same issues and the same ideas were being offered in a form only slightly modified from the past, perhaps with the addition of a little more urgency. The board's preliminary discussions felt muted. How could this be when their field was in a period of extremely rapid change and some aspects of the work they tried to support were at risk? They finally shifted their discussion away from internal matters to an assessment of the larger arena in which the association operated. It was clear to them that their profession needed stronger, more aggressive leadership to help manage the changes taking place and to defend the profession with vigor against the threats it faced. As they talked, their conviction grew that the association should play that role.

This was an easier agreement to reach than it would be to achieve. To assume a more visible leadership role would be seen by other organizations as a threat. To move ahead with this decision would be challenging not only for the staff, who would face resistance on a daily basis, but also for the board, which would have to explain the decision, defend it, and support the staff and each other as they acted to make it happen. The board was resolved to tackle these issues head-on.

After arriving at this critical insight into the role they desired the association to play, the board found that the balance of the plan fell into place. Interestingly, the objectives and many of the proposed action items in the emerging plan were not very different from those in the draft document that was the retreat's starting point. What was different was the frame of reference the board had established for the plan, a set of decisions that only the board could bring together and approve.

The new plan made an important declaration that set a standard throughout the plan for measuring results. At the end of the day, the association had more than a management tool. The board had created a leadership document that added value to the field, that shaped the board's role in the coming years, that enabled the staff to act more confidently in pursuing its work, and that clarified decision making as the organization's assets were deployed.

Good plans resemble each other in a number of ways. First, a good plan is legible; everyone can read it and understand it. It also feels smart, not out of touch with the reality everyone knows. It feels inevitable, as though the organization has no choice but to move in a particular direction. Last, and most important, it gives everyone, including the board, a part in the success of the plan, a success that can be measured, tasted, savored, and celebrated.

There is immeasurable value in a plan that actively engages the board in its development and holds the board accountable for a part of its success. At the least, it gives the board a deeper understanding of what the mission requires and what good work looks like, in terms of both its difficulty and its results. At the most, it builds the board's sense of ownership and accomplishment, which are essential if board members are to use the plan to make decisions and are expected to help with fund raising.

EVALUATION

With a good plan in place, a board has the basis and the context for judging results. Some plans imply results, others spell them out. A plan that does not allow for clear measurements of progress will vanish over time, useless to the staff and forgotten by the board, a candidate for that prized spot on the shelf behind the director's desk.

Evaluation is a critical part of a board's work, but it is an exceptionally difficult task for most boards to perform. We are still prone to equate evaluation with judgment rather than learning. The process is still closely linked in our minds with punishment, and if few people want to dish it out, fewer still want to take it. Boards are trapped by this attitude. If board members like the staff and feel they genuinely do a good job, they will avoid evaluation out of a fear that the process might be perceived as a lack of confidence. If a board is struggling with the staff, it may be equally resistant to evaluation so as to avoid coming to grips with the need to take definitive action— or, put more forcefully, the need to take responsibility.

Responsibility is at the heart of evaluation. The board is responsible for results. If the mission matters, if the organization has value, then the board must direct its energies to seeing that the mission is accomplished. The earlier discussions on fiscal accountability and on planning depend for their meaning on the board's ability to use both activities to engage in regular evaluation.

Staff are often complicit in the board's inability to engage in evaluation, sometimes for good reason. Because they have substantial responsibility to achieve results, they have the burden of getting the job done. Because they have access to the data that document results, they shape how results are reported and presented. While to others this may look like control, to the staff it can be the beginning of immobilizing insecurity.

Staff have a sharp appreciation of how difficult results can be to achieve, and may lack faith in their ability to achieve them. Even if the goals are realistic and exciting, staff may back away if any perceived failure or shortcoming poses a risk to job security or peace of mind. Staff share the aversion to being judged that is common to us all and will go to great lengths to avoid it if they can. If the board is unreliable in any way, the staff will skirt the process at every opportunity. If the board fails to differentiate between evaluation and judgment, the information the staff shares with the board will be carefully screened to minimize potential bad news or disappointments.

It is important to shed the negative associations that stymie evaluation. Evaluation is about learning. The process should ask not only "what happened?" but also "what can we learn?" To be useful, evaluation requires that some agreement about results be in place. Was the goal this year to serve more people? How many more? Were we interested in achieving economies of scale, or had we decided to spend more on fewer people in the hopes of seeing more profound results? How will we measure those results? Each question implies a way to find the answer, either in the budget and the analysis that went into it, or in the plan and the decisions that it embodies.

The agreements among board members and staff about the results being sought should be given "voice" in tangible, explicit ways, or some combination of chaos and inaction will develop. The phrase "it goes without saying" must be banished from the script. Evaluation is not a mind reader's game; things have to be spelled out. Without that, evaluation has no anchor. The process will shift from place to place and topic to topic based on the hobbyhorses and idiosyncrasies of individual board members. The board will resemble a gang of Goldilocks running around the bears' house, each murmuring about the porridge before shifting to a discussion of the beds. It is this vision of random, ill-informed tasting and testing that makes the specter of a board engaged in evaluation such a nightmare to staff.

What creates the climate for good evaluation? In addition to having agreed on the results being sought, the board has to regularize and formalize its approach to evaluation in a way that allows the staff to support the process. The board's work and the staff's work must find common links in the plan itself. What are the best intervals for measuring results in key areas? Once determined, they need to be slotted into the planning agenda for the board's meetings. How will results be presented? Staff need to work, sometimes with a board committee, to determine what data and information tell the clearest story and generate the best questions. Should the director present key findings, or should the responsible staff team play a primary part? How do we approach a presentation to the board that is not a recitation of the written material but instead builds on it?

What if the results are disappointing? This is where an effective board distinguishes itself. The issue is less what did *you* (the staff) do wrong than what could *we* have done differently? How can we do it better? A tougher question to ask and answer is whether to continue to try. Sometimes results tell us what can't be done or what may have to be done by an organization other than our own. No evaluation is free of risk—to our self-confidence, to our skill as planners, to our sense of possibility—but the risk must be placed at an acceptable level and then taken.

Evaluation is occurring all the time, whether it is formalized or not. People are always forming opinions and drawing conclusions. The virtue of approaching evaluation seriously and systematically is that we harness all that potentially random and dangerous opinion forming in a manner that is constructive to the organization and is transparent to everyone.

FUND RAISING

At last, fund raising.

Most executive directors long for a board that will do it, and are regularly disappointed in their hopes. All board members, if pressed, feel guilty that they are not doing more, and wish they could.

There must be people out there doing it successfully. The *Chronicle of Philanthropy* reported that giving was up again in 1999; $190 billion was given to charity, a seven percent increase over 1998. Clearly, someone is asking; more clearly still, a lot of people are giving. It is just not clear how much of the asking can be credited to board members.

There are boards designed to raise money. They are typically the boards of large organizations with board members who have been carefully selected with giving and getting in mind. Then there are the vast majority of boards in which current experience with fund raising is limited but expectations are rising.

Having experience with fund raising and possessing a high net worth are contributing factors to a board member's success in this area. They are not the only indicators; in fact, they are sometimes highly unreliable. It is disappointing verging on maddening to discover that the board member carefully chosen because he looked like the perfect donor and fund raiser is both those things . . . for another organization.

This leads to the first requirement where boards and fund raising are concerned: being clear about expectations. If board members are expected to be personally generous, that ought to be stated during the recruitment stage, not at the orientation. If board members are expected to participate in fund raising, that must also be clearly spelled out and some thought given to what it will actually mean. Is the organization about to begin a capital campaign, or are board members asked to play a modest part in the annual giving campaign? Is the organization trying to approach individuals for substantial contributions, or trying to get current donors to increase their levels of support? At the end of the year, how much is the board—in total—expected to have helped raise? What about individual results?

Executive directors and development staff often want their boards to do more but then fail to identify activities at which the board stands a chance of succeeding. Boards have a limited repertoire of appropriate fund-raising activities: individual donor solicitation of various kinds, special events, an ability to open a few doors, and a tag-along value on fund-raising calls to corporations and foundations. Few board members can call directly on a CEO for corporate support; most of those requests are channeled through a grant-making program within the company that is designed for staff-to-staff contact. Building a fund-raising strategy that requires unrealistic board behavior will fail. A little less dreaming and a little more reality have to be introduced by staff into their fund-raising plans for the board.

If we accept that the role might be more limited than we imagined, there is still a great gulf between forming a realistic expectation about board fund raising and watching boards do it successfully.

Asking for money is perhaps the hardest thing in the world to do. It leaves everyone vulnerable to hearing the most depressing word in the English language: no. According to the schoolyard chant, words will never hurt us—but the person who came up with that rhyme never asked anyone for money.

There is only one thing that will get us over the fear of asking, and it is not training or practice, although they will help eventually. The one thing that will take a board member right up to the line and help him cross it is a belief in the power of the mission that overcomes all doubt and hesitation, a clear understanding of what the organization does that makes a difference for the good. That is a tall order. It is not an order that will be filled by a board member who never comes to meetings, isn't prepared when she gets there, leaves early, fails to make the committee meeting, hasn't contributed personally quite yet, and can't clear the calendar for the planning retreat.

The only board member who can achieve vertical takeoff on the matter of fund raising is a board member who is fully committed to the organization, has found a part of its work that has meaning for him, can connect his work on the board with the success of the organization, understands what the money will be used for, and can assure the fund-raising prospect that the money will be well spent. In other words, a conscientious member of a board that works.

With that as a foundation, a board member can go on to master the details of fund raising, learn to make a formal case, and get to the point where a dollar amount doesn't bring on a case of the stutters. Without that, there is much remedial work to be done.

It does not matter who is on your board. Adding new people with high net worth or corporate connections to replace more modestly endowed members does not translate into effective fund raising. Those people require what everyone else needs—a reason to risk rejection. Some of the most powerful fund raisers are people who have benefited directly from what an organization does. An African-American woman on the board of a local YWCA was given five calls to make on potential donors. She hesitated to do it. She was not a wealthy woman. She had no experience asking for money. She didn't know the people she was approaching. She wasn't certain what to say. The development officer asked her how important the Y had been to her growing up in the neighborhood, what kind of difference it still made in the lives of girls who lived nearby, how important to her and to them it was that the Y had the money to reach out and serve more young people. The board member had the answers to all of those questions in a way that another board member with more affluence or a different history might not. From that moment, she never hesitated to ask for money, and never had to feel guilty that she wasn't doing as much as she might to help the organization find the resources to do its work.

Fund raising is not the starting point for building board capacity, but it can be a way to gauge that capacity. If a board addresses the fundamentals of its role and improves the way it works and the quality of its work, then success in fund raising is within reach. A poorly organized and poorly motivated board will never be promising raw material for the task.

Even with a strong foundation and an urgent need for resources, it is important to build a little forgiveness into the expectation that all members of the board will be fund raisers. By defining success with a tolerance for variations in skill, temperament, and culture, all board members can feel competent, even if not all will ask for a big gift. A board member who came up in life treading a very tough path and made it a rule never to ask anyone for anything was generous about sharing her relationships in the community but refused to ever ask anyone for money. Under any reasonable definition, she would have to be counted a successful fund raiser.

CONCLUSION

The variety among nonprofits means an equal variety in the detail and emphasis of board work. Each board has to think about how it adds value to the organization and meets its essential obligations. Because executive directors struggle hard to find the resources to keep their organizations afloat, they are desperate to place fund raising at the center of the board's role. Certainly, they are entitled to feel this way, and every board member should vow to do her best. But in the rush to raise funds, other tasks cannot be ignored. A few activities by their nature help a board to be an asset to the organization. They also help a board to meet its obligations to the public. There may be differences among organizations about the best ways to present financial information and the most appropriate ways to plan and evaluate, but these functions must find competence at the board level in almost every organization if the board is to do its part. These are not necessarily the most glamorous of board functions or the easiest to master, but they are the best opportunities a board has to make a difference.

CHAPTER 6

Building Productivity through Board Culture

A colleague describes the peer pressure to be found in the boardroom as just as fierce as that of any teenage gang. She is only slightly exaggerating. Even with a decent orientation to board service, a new board member will spend the first few board meetings searching carefully for important clues to the board's behavior. Does everyone arrive on time, or is there an assumption that the meeting will begin 10 or 15 minutes late? Do we stick to the agenda or do we wander? When the meeting wanders, does everyone join in, or is this a cause for exasperation? Who looks exasperated? Is this someone I want to impress? Is there pressure from the chair to stay on schedule, or should I ask my family to leave a light on for me on the nights the board meets? Am I sitting at the right place at the table, or have I landed in Siberia? How can I figure out what everyone is talking about without asking a question that will reveal me as hopelessly out of the loop?

None of these pressing questions is addressed during the typical orientation, yet each in its way is important to have answered.

Every board has its rules of conduct and not all of them can be found in writing. Some are the products of history and habit, and others reflect the power of personalities to shape behavior. When history and habit have been benign, the greatest downside may be the length of time it takes the board to realize that its luncheon meeting, scheduled for years for the first Thursday of the month, no longer works for a significant number of board members. When history and habit have been less benign, it may mean that board members suit up for meetings as though for a wrestling match, because that behavior has been tolerated long enough for it to become the norm.

Respecting tradition is important; being trapped by it has little value. Giving individuals room to express their viewpoints candidly is highly desirable; being held hostage to someone's relentless determination to prevail is not.

To make the work of the board rewarding for the organization and satisfying for individual members can be a challenge that individual board members are unprepared to accept. A board member faced with inefficiency or acrimony will more often withdraw than attempt to change the status quo. Board service is a voluntary activity. How much time and energy can a board member be expected to commit to taking on his or her peers? Board service also sometimes involves overlapping relationships among members. Is it smart to challenge someone's behavior in one setting when a day later the individual will be encountered at a social event, at church services, or in another boardroom?

A board's culture—its way of doing business and the nuance of its behavior when members come together—is where the fallible, human aspect of governance is most on display. The board may appear to be a conceptually unified entity, but it is in fact an assortment of individuals who trail their personalities into the boardroom along with their skills and experience. With luck and a little effort, board members can put to one side the need to assert their individuality in the pursuit of a common commitment to the mission. It is unreasonable to expect perfect self-effacement, but it is not unreasonable to hope that a self-conscious effort will be made by everyone to be as good as possible.

The good news is that culture is not fixed; it can change and evolve. It can see a better way to work and adopt it, and it can differentiate between a healthy difference of opinion and a war of attrition, saying yes to one and no to the other. A board's culture does not have to represent the group's default settings, the behavior it reproduces from habit rather than reflection. Like every human enterprise, there is not just room for improvement but a way to achieve it. Good habits can be affirmed; bad habits can be broken. Finally, new habits can be learned if it is in the best interest of the organization that things should change. The test for any change is always what is best for the organization.

Nevertheless, the power of the peer group is formidable. While board members might rise up as a group and decide it is time to rethink the way they work and relate to each other, it is not a likely scenario. That is why it is useful to examine the issue of board culture through the prism of board leadership. The impulse to change has its best chance of succeeding if it either originates with the chair or finds its strongest support there. Sadly, it has its least chance of succeeding if the banner is carried alone or too vigorously by the executive director. The board has a delicate but deep sense of its prerogatives, including a finely tuned, if sometimes misdirected, sense of who is in charge. As well-intentioned and knowledgeable as the executive director might be about the process of board development, the final responsibility for the quality of a board's performance rests with the board and with its leadership. For that reason, the board chair has as one of his or her chief assignments the important job of creating and maintaining the most effective board possible and the culture to support it.

LEADING THE BOARD

A paradox of nonprofit governance is that legal accountability and the welfare of an organization are vested with a group of part-time volunteers. The first challenge for any nonprofit is to find a group of qualified, dedicated people willing to play this role. The second challenge is to find someone in the group willing to be the chair. (The third challenge is finding someone willing to be the treasurer, a problem addressed elsewhere in this book.)

The challenges of chairing a board are well known and the board meeting is just the tip of the iceberg. Clearly, board leadership has to be cultivated so that good leadership will be continuously available to the organization. In fact, the very first responsibility of a new board chair is to find a successor, or better yet, a couple of successors, given the unpredictability of life. The second responsibility of the board chair is to make the job appear within the reach of mere mortals, so that prospective leaders who have talent but also concerns about finding the time and the patience to do it well will see it as a job that can be done.

As a general rule, it is good to have the chair in place for at least two years. In some organizations, the term is only a year, but in those instances, there is often a system that simultaneously identifies the chair-elect and allows the immediate past chair to continue as a member of the board. This three-year leadership arc enables a velocity in board leadership that is highly valued in some organizations while at the same time preserving continuity.

Because a good board chair is such a critical but difficult asset to recruit, there are many boards where the chair can be reelected without limit. This is a harder model to accept as good practice, although just enough shining examples of long-term chairs exist to tempt putting good practice aside. The board chair of a large history museum, for example, held the position for 15 years. He was an extraordinarily temperate but firm leader, and dedicated a substantial amount of time to learning what he needed to know to continue to provide valuable service to the board and to the organization. Among his many achievements, he became quite adept at government relations, an area where experience counts. In this arena, he assisted not only his own museum but also hundreds of others. Before he retired from his position as chair, he oversaw a difficult merger and the recruitment of a new executive director. When those tasks were completed, he stepped down to become one of many good board members.

During his tenure, his fellow board members were very happy to let him continue for as long as he liked. Lucky for them and for the organization, he was a very gifted and wise person. Such luck, when it happens, is to be treasured, but luck is not something a board can rely upon; good practice provides a stronger safety net.

There have been experiments with joint, shared, or collaborative leadership models for nonprofit boards, and a number have been quite successful. Their success is often linked to the first set of personalities to attempt the arrangement, and to the degree to which they managed to negotiate the responsibilities and work load so that the divisions were clear to the board and functional for the executive director. A national women's media organization used co-chairs to make the assignment more manageable and to achieve representation of print and broadcast media at a highly visible leadership level that advanced the work of the organization. The first pair of women to serve as co-chairs created a positive template for their successors, including a confident working relationship with the executive director. A failure to achieve even one of these benefits would have made the model difficult to sustain.

MODELING GOOD BEHAVIOR

A good chair takes the job seriously and conveys that serious-ness of purpose to others on the board. Healthy boards often describe themselves as working hard but knowing how to have fun. Their priorities are clear and the board chair has helped to keep them front and center. The work of the board is care-fully planned and structured to get it done, whether at board meetings, through committee assignments, or through support for the staff. Board members feel mutual accountability to each other and the chair that perpetuates productivity and makes their work together a pleasure (if not fun). At the end of a year, a board with the benefit of good leadership can see the results of its work in the life of the organization and take satisfaction from that. It also knows what fell short and why so that remedial action, even if difficult, can be taken.

In the course of building a high-functioning board culture, the chair needs to create and sustain good will and trust in the boardroom and in the director's office. Good will and trust are important to have in the ordinary course of events, but they are essential when an organization faces difficult decisions. As long as people trust each other to be honest and motivated by what's best for the organization, disagreements can be resolved honorably and tough decisions can be made. To achieve this level of good will, a good chair gives everyone on the board his or her voice, invites discussion, listens for consensus, and discourages those with the tendency to hijack a debate.

OVERRULING THE UNRULY

The toughest governance challenge facing any organization—not just the board, but also the staff—is the unruly or disaf-fected board member. This person can take many forms. There are bullies, showoffs, the righteously indignant, the dumb, the dumber, and the slackers. They do not need to be loud to be disruptive. Some are lethally subtle as they go along their demoralizing way. They uniformly fail to have a sense of boundaries, and either lack the capacity, or just don't care, to understand how their behavior affects the rest of the group.

Complicating the board's response to such personalities is the recognition that they often mean well. One organization in a transition from a period of fiscal anxiety to one with a strong prospect of growth was trapped by the residual fears of the board members who recalled the earlier era when times were tough. To the new executive director's chagrin and to the bafflement of many on the board, a small group of veterans insisted that the sky would fall, was probably already falling and no one but they realized it yet. In budget deliberations, they insisted on the most punishing estimates of income in the name of fiscal conservatism. They couldn't be placated or reassured. As time went on, other board members became more and more withdrawn at meetings and more and more vocal in the parking lot and on the phone the next day. No one doubted the sincerity of their unruly peers, and no one was ready to take them on.

This is not an unusual pattern of behavior when an individual board member or a group of board members begins to dominate the board's work. By sitting quietly, praying that the meeting will end soon, board members effectively cede their power to the least constructive member of the group. Bad behavior doesn't even have to be loud to be debilitating. Board members who regularly fail to attend meetings, making quorums difficult to achieve, also effectively incapacitate the board. To a lesser but still serious degree, board members who fail to prepare for meetings, making it necessary for meetings to become tutorials, are as guilty as the unruly in undermining the board.

The damage can quickly spread beyond the board to the staff. The disparity in power that exists between the board and the staff, particularly the board and the executive director, can be an overwhelming temptation to a board member inclined to be a bully. If peers are off limits, the staff is not. What an ugly scene it is when a board member takes off on the executive director during a meeting, as board members sit silently like witnesses at a car accident. Not the best way to build trust and good will, but definitely effective if the only goal is to demonstrate who has power and who is powerless.

Finding the will to deal with unruly board members is extremely difficult, but failing to do it makes everyone complicit in the dysfunction that results. The first line of defense for the board when faced by this problem is the board chair. The chair needs to have the courage to correct, admonish, corral, and sometimes suggest retirement to unruly members. Failing that (and it is a very serious failure), board members need to find the courage to speak up in defense of themselves. This may involve a little practice before a mirror and the recruitment of an ally or two among the other board members. It is hard to say: "I disagree with you and I believe I am not alone. We understand your position but we need to bring this discussion to a close and make a decision." Or, "I have problems with putting the staff on the spot this way. It is unfair to them and not productive for us." If it were easy to do this, it would be done routinely. It is not easy, but no board can survive a toxic board culture for long.

Election or appointment to the board is not a binding contract. Some people are not cut out for board service. They may lack the capacity to work collectively with others; they may be unable to adapt to new settings; they may lack the mental acuity to tackle complexity; or they may just be too lazy to do the work. When the problem surfaces, it must be dealt with. If their terms are up for renewal, the nominating committee should refrain from inviting them back. If that legitimate option is not available, asking people to resign by pointing out how at odds they are with the direction of the rest of the board or the organization is certainly kinder and more straightforward than dusting off the bylaws and cranking up the recall procedure—but that option should not be eliminated if that is what it will take.

Board members do not have to put up with bad behavior and they won't. Their time and their peace of mind are too valuable to sacrifice. Unlike their unruly peers, good board members leave all the time. Strong board leadership and a sense of obligation and commitment to the organization can control the threat that a disruptive or unproductive board member presents to a productive board culture.

GORGEOUS MONSTERS

In a separate category from the unruly but often as perplexing to the work of the board, are founders. These can be founding board members or the founding executive director or some combination; but whatever the configuration, founders present unique challenges to an organization's development and the board's capacity to adapt itself to different circumstances and needs.

The qualities that make founders successful are the same qualities that can confound an organization at later stages of development. Beginning a nonprofit is a daunting enterprise; it takes conviction, energy, passion, stubbornness, and a great talent for persuasion. Founders are absolutely persuaded by what they are doing; they have no doubts. This focus is often allied with a charm and charisma that make people forget themselves and say yes. People asked for money say yes, and people asked to serve on the board say yes. It is possible that founders lack a genetic capacity to hear the word no or its synonyms.

Founders are gorgeous and seductive. We feel rewarded by their attention and faith in us. We are flattered that they have asked for our help. We forgive them if they are a little excessive—after all, it is in pursuit of a good cause. We overlook the things they are not good at because those things do not matter as much as the things at which they are geniuses. Where would the nonprofit sector be without founders?

The success and power of founders make it that much harder to admit when an organization needs a different kind of energy or set of talents than those that launched it. Some founders are wise in addition to being gorgeous and seductive, and either grow to meet new challenges or cultivate the next generation of leadership needed to sustain success. Others—too many others—lack the personal insight to appreciate their limits, or come to depend too much on the power and admiration that go with their position to give them up.

The transitions are never easy to negotiate. When a founder, who had labored without compensation, finally pulled together sufficient funding to hire a staff, she became the organization's first executive director. Shortly after moving to the position of paid staff, she realized that, technically, the board she had recruited now had the power to remove her as the executive director. Although this was an unlikely turn of events, she was not the kind of person who left such things to chance, so she began to look into amending the bylaws in a way that would eliminate the board's right to terminate her. She was very surprised at the objections the board raised to having this responsibility taken from it. Although they too felt there was only a remote possibility that they would want to fire her, they forcefully resisted her efforts to abridge their role. They were not the most independent board in town, but neither were they the director's amen chorus. They understood their obligation to be stewards of the organization and not merely grateful supporters of the founder.

This board's dilemma is the dilemma of any board faced with founders who are unable to understand the limits of their claim on the organization. Once the organization has established its value and attracted the support and credibility of donors, clients, and staff, the best interests and the needs of the organization must dominate decision making, not the will of the founder.

Board members who find themselves in the middle of problems either linked directly to founders or compounded by them need as much courage as they would if tackling a purely unruly board member. Gratitude, admiration, and kindness can complicate the board's ability to do what is right. Nevertheless, it is the board's responsibility to do the right thing. Interestingly enough, because the board chair is so often a founder, the board chair is not the automatic problem solver in this situation. Instead, it usually requires a coalition of board members who are ready not just to raise the issue, but also to commit to solving the problem. This may mean giving more time to the organization than before, or stepping up to play greater leadership roles to offset the diminished role of the founder, but merely raising the issue won't do the trick.

Whatever the requirements for a successful transition turn out to be, a board either works to solve the problem or acquiesces in the organization's stagnation. An organization may manage to maintain its momentum with a board culture that functions as a cult of personality, but that success will be short-lived.

RESOLVING CONFLICT

Good board leadership, a strong commitment to reward constructive board service, and a drive to maintain the independence of the board all contribute to a positive board culture.

These should be allied with a board's healthy respect for conflict and equally healthy mechanisms for reaching agreement.

Conflict is natural in a board. It is not just that people will disagree; boards invite conflict each time new people join the board. It is inevitable, when a board identifies new skills and perspectives for inclusion on the board, that those who join will challenge the status quo. A board that recruits people with business skills should not be surprised if there is pressure to do some things in a more businesslike way. A board that strives for diversity after an extended period of relative homogeneity needs to be prepared for the conflicts that absorbing and capitalizing on diversity will bring and see them as healthy.

Boards engaged in meaningful work are also by definition engaged in complicated and absorbing work. When the rubber stamps are put away, a board will find itself with much more to talk about and disagree about than in the past.

To make the most of what conflict can represent and to avoid useless wrangling, the board needs to adopt a few boundaries for itself. One of the best is a rule that all issues are placed on the table, not under it. By honoring this rule, the board consolidates its authority to reach decisions that relate to its legal responsibilities and duties to the organization. The rule eliminates any maverick instincts among individual board members and reduces the temptation to form alliances to achieve a partisan, preordained result. People are asked to speak up and speak clearly so that all points of views, concerns, and objections are put where everyone on the board can consider their merits and weigh their value. The hallway, the parking lot, the phone call are not productive places to carry on a discussion that should concern and involve the entire board.

This rule argues for a very careful use of the executive committee, if one exists. An executive committee, like other committees of the board, can be helpful in framing issues and in doing preliminary research on the best course of action. Good committee work, including the work of the executive committee, can flatten the learning curve for the board and allow it to address the heart of an issue. Still, a committee never relieves the board of its responsibility to make decisions.

An executive committee is not a convenient mechanism for avoiding the full board or usurping its role. It may be easier to achieve a result with a smaller group than with a larger one, but in matters of governance it can be a form of cheating. How incompetent is the board that it cannot deal with complexity and doesn't know how to conduct itself during a full-ranging discussion? How did it get to be this unreliable? A contributing factor may have been an unwillingness to address the board's deficiencies and make it strong enough to do its work. In this situation, the easy solution is to shift the real work of governance to the more manageable and (not surprisingly) better prepared executive committee. This solution may backfire if the board perceives the extent to which it has been marginalized and members make a bid to regain their legal authority. This is guaranteed to be a conflict that will require every ounce of leadership, skill, and good will to resolve.

The other rule for keeping conflict healthy belongs to the board chair. The chair needs to establish a ground rule that all opinions will be respected and listened to because the only motive in stating an opinion or taking a position is the best interest of the organization. This ground rule has the effect of immediately elevating the discussion to the right level. While the best interest of the organization should be the only motivation in taking a position, human nature being what it is, representational politics being what it is, there is a probability that not all motives will be pure. The ground rule has the effect of placing people on warning that they need to play fair by the organization. It also requires that board members listen carefully and respectfully to all that is said.

The final rule also belongs to the board chair. The chair needs to make sure that everyone, and not just the most aggressive few, has a chance to voice their opinions. This requires explicitly inviting people to speak and also summarizing the trend of the discussion at intervals along the way to see how much agreement is evident within the group. Summarizing the trend of the discussion has a few additional benefits. It helps to reduce the amount of repetition that can occur when people have strong opinions and are only happy if they hear themselves expressing them. It also allows the chair to test to see if a consensus is developing that makes the moment to ask formally for a decision clearer.

There is an argument to be made in favor of using a consensus model when particularly difficult or contentious issues come before the board, even when an organization uses a more formal decision-making structure, such as *Roberts' Rules of Order*. Seeking consensus inevitably lengthens the time spent on discussion, but people tend to value the opportunity to come to general agreement more than they value the efficiency of a vote. The voting process can create a class of winners and losers, a sense that one position prevailed over another, which with difficult decisions can be counterproductive. Consensus requires that people accept a decision and support it, even if they do not entirely agree with it. It is the element of acceptance that gives consensus greater psychological power when a difficult decision is reached. Good decision making is often undermined when board members who feel as though they "lost" take those feelings into the community or the membership and try to sustain debate by diminishing the authority of the board's decision or the quality of the deliberations that led to the decision. Suspending traditional voting and shifting decision-making structures may not forestall a board member who is determined to be a hero at the expense of the board's authority, but it may be helpful enough to be worth raising with the board, along with the reasons why.

CONCLUSION

Many things contribute to board productivity, but the power of the board's culture to create the environment in which good work is possible should not be underestimated. The new board member at the beginning of the chapter, who is trying to read between the lines and be accepted by the group, would find a board with a good chair a reassuring and satisfying place to spend precious time.

Certainly, with the support and leadership of a good chair, she will feel protected from the distractions of self-obsessed and time-wasting fellow board members, and know that if the board needs to made a tough decision, board members trust each other to make a thoughtful and deliberate one. One of the ways in which a chair can measure his or her success is the extent to which other board members feel they are involved in contributing meaningfully to the board's work and the organization's well-being. A good board culture supports the board's productivity and heightens the satisfaction board members take in their service.

CHAPTER 7

A Working Partnership: The Executive Director and the Board

Like the tango, the relationship between the executive director and the board requires a strong sense of balance, a high degree of trust, a willingness to follow as well as lead, and an ability to communicate clearly, sometimes subtly, throughout the course of the dance. Partners must temper concentration on their own movements with an awareness of what is taking place around them. They also need to understand and respect the form. The tango is not the twist. Although there is room for originality and invention, there are a handful of conventions, traditions, and agreements that must be acknowledged and honored.

The relationship between the executive director and the board is one of the most complex and perplexing relationships in the nonprofit sector. Who is in charge? Who does what? Who gets to lead and who gets to follow? The fact that the

---

Parts of this chapter appear in *The Chief Executive's Role in Developing the Board* (1998) and are published here with the permission of the National Center for Nonprofit Boards.

answer to these questions is often "it depends" does little to reassure the executive director whose survival often requires getting the answer right the first time.

Complicating the matter is the nature of the board itself. A board is not a fixed and tidy object in a nonprofit organization. In fact, it is very untidy. The board has a nature, but so do all of its parts. Some of the parts are wise and some naïve; some are energetic and some passive; some master all the steps and others have two left feet. The executive director must contend with all of this.

Trying to simplify the complications of the relationship by declaring that the board governs and the staff manages, or the board makes policy and the staff administers it fails more often than it works. These formulations have the simplicity of slogans, but trying to use them can be time-consuming, anxiety-producing, and fundamentally counterproductive. Are there differences between what the board does and what staff is responsible for? Absolutely. Are the differences constant and immutable? Absolutely not. By seeking clarity through over-simplification, the traditional formulation creates artificial boundaries that fail to acknowledge an organization's stage of development, the size of its staff, or the skill of its staff, not to mention the skill of its board.

Even the common way of expressing this theory of the relationship—governance *versus* management—implies inherent opposition and creates artificial boundaries. Board members and executive directors exhaust valuable good will policing the boundaries between policy and administration, searching for infractions. The insistence on a sharp differentiation leads to a transgressor model of board/staff relations where boundaries are often only revealed because one party or the other feels the boundaries have been breached. The losers in these boundary disputes are always the executive director and the organization everyone has pledged to serve. The latter is reason enough to find ways to make the relationship successful, but the additional incentive of an executive director's self-preservation can also be a positive force if used correctly.

The key to a successful relationship between the board and the executive director is the care with which the director helps the board to be a good partner. In the unique calculus of the nonprofit sector, a stronger board does not automatically come at the expense of the executive director's authority or autonomy. The more effort a director makes to develop a board that works and works well, the stronger the underlying relationship will be between the board and the staff, and the more confidence and respect the board will have in the director's work.

Although in the final analysis boards get better because they want to, there are numerous ways in which an executive director can contribute to building the board's effectiveness. It is in the director's self-interest, and certainly in the organization's best interest, for the director to be an active participant in the process of building an effective and high-functioning board.

FULLY VALUE THE BOARD

Rather than feeling outnumbered by the board, the smart executive director sees the board and its membership strategically as a way to leverage talent, resources, and energy on behalf of the organization. Luckily, boards also prefer to see themselves as talented, resourceful, and energetic, and, on that basis, will welcome the chance to put those qualities to work.

While it is useful to view the board strategically, it is also important for the executive director to enjoy working with the board. The director needs to like the board, or at a minimum see among its members people he or she appreciates and values the chance to work with. At the heart of good board and staff relations is a genuine pleasure in working together. The pleasure is not just personal; it is linked to the sense of satisfaction that comes from a good job done well, and done together. The natural byproducts of this collegiality are the basic trust and good will needed by everyone involved to do complicated business in challenging times.

UNDERSTAND AND EXERCISE AUTHORITY

To support the board and help develop its capacity, an executive director has to be confident about her role in the organization and comfortable with her authority. Within the nonprofit sector, we have developed a useful and devastating description for boards that overstep their role and meddle in management and administrative matters: micromanaging. The field has been slower to coin a phrase that captures as neatly the problem presented by uncertain or tentative management. Assuming that the board has hired the right person for the job, executive directors help themselves and help their boards by having the confidence to do their jobs. An executive director may feel less exposed or vulnerable to second-guessing if the board can be made to own a piece of every decision, but this approach is doomed from the start. Some of the confusion about who does what in an organization might be resolved if executive directors were clearer in their own minds about what they have been given the authority and, therefore, the responsibility to do.

As was noted in an earlier chapter, boards work on what is in front of them. Executive directors have a lot of discretion over what comes before the board. If the director brings management and administrative issues to the board, the board assumes that these issues are theirs to work on. When this happens, it is disingenuous to complain that the board is micromanaging. A board is better and works harder if the executive director keeps the board's agenda clear of tasks that don't belong to it.

Some of the confusion over who does what, can be avoided if the executive director has an up-to-date job description that the board understands and supports, and an annual performance appraisal that clarifies expectations and rationalizes evaluation. It is also very helpful to have on the board someone who periodically questions the board's involvement in a decision and redirects it to the staff. There are few words sweeter in the language of board/staff relations than "Isn't this something the staff should decide?" If a natural talent for this does not emerge among board members, this is a useful piece of coaching for the director to undertake with the chair.

BUILD A STRONG RELATIONSHIP WITH THE CHAIR

An executive director has no stronger ally on the board than the chair and no more potent advocate for building a board that works. In fact, the relationship with the chair sets the tone for the executive director's relationship with the board and serves as a model for the behavior of other board members toward the director and the staff.

Ideally, the chair is a safe place for the executive director to seek advice and to raise concerns. The executive director needs to trust the chair and the chair, in turn, needs to trust the executive director. The confidence they have in each other must be sufficient to build a productive working relationship, but not so great that other board members or the board as a whole feel there is a charmed circle from which they have been excluded.

Given the typical turnover in the position of chair, an executive director should be ready to accommodate the different working styles of those who take the position, and develop ways to make the most of the relationship. The director is also well advised to consider it a part of his or her job to make the job of chair one that others will be willing to do when the time comes. This means helping the current chair to have a productive experience, and by extension, making the assignment easy for qualified successors to say yes to. As disconcerting as it may be to have to readjust working arrangements every few years to accommodate a new chair, it is far more difficult to work for longer than necessary with a challenging chair, or to have a series of chairs who have been pressed into service whether they show a talent for the role or not.

A critical element in the working relationship with the chair is the willingness to establish strong lines of communications. These can be formal, such as a standing phone appointment or breakfast meeting, or more informal, but they should be regular and carefully thought through.

The one communication with the board chair that can never be neglected is the review of the agenda prior to a board meeting. The chair is not a bit player in the board meeting, but the manager of it. To play that part successfully, the executive director and the board chair need to review the agenda carefully, and the director must be sure that there is sufficient support, written information, or access to senior staff for the chair to be prepared for the meeting. The more confident the chair's management of the board meeting, the more effective and confident the board.

Even in the most productive relationships, there will be moments when tensions or disagreements arise. While tension in a stress-filled life is usually better avoided, periodic tension between a director and the chair of the board is natural and often a healthy sign. Blessed with a good executive director, a board can become complacent, and give up its responsibilities in the face of the director's reassuring competence. An executive director needs to accept that disagreements with the chair (and other members of the board) are likely to come up, and that these moments shouldn't be avoided. The impulse to underplay bad news, selectively present information, or fail to raise important issues in order to avoid rocking the boat with the chair may work in the short run, but will fail in the long term. Concealing information undermines the confidence that the director and chair must have in each other. The rule is "no surprises" and it is always in effect.

CULTIVATE LEADERSHIP AMONG BOARD MEMBERS

Continuity of leadership and of performance matters not only at the staff level, but also at the board level. The pattern of strong staff leadership and gradually weakening board leadership may look useful to a shortsighted director, but it harms the organization and handicaps the director when the moment inevitably arises that calls for a strong board and an effective chair.

An important consideration in building leadership among board members is that competent chairs are made, not born. They do not rise from the mist just as they are needed. Ideally, a board will have candidates both willing and able to lead when the time comes. If leadership within the board is broadly cultivated, the board will yield strong candidates. The bigger challenge is getting good people to say yes to serving as chair. In this respect, the executive director can play an important part by being a good partner, someone ready to help the chair do a good job and help the board work effectively.

PARTICIPATE IN BOARD RECRUITMENT

Let's return briefly to the dance metaphor that opened this chapter. It may be exciting just to show up alone at a dance and let fate take a hand, but it is a high-risk strategy for an executive director. The executive director needs to take an active and appropriate role in identifying, cultivating, and recruiting new board members. This requires that the director place a high value on the importance of having an active and vigorously led nominating committee, and encourage the chair to do the same.

At every turn, the nominating or board development committee needs the full support and encouragement of the executive director, including a regular stream of suggestions about potential candidates and enterprising approaches to the cultivation of prospects. Board members serve for long enough to make their careful cultivation and selection worthwhile. A two- or three-year term will seem a life term to the executive director and to other board members if candidates are chosen without thought or preparation.

SHAPE BOARD ORIENTATION

Although board members are ultimately responsible for understanding their role, an orientation program expedites the process and guarantees that every member of the board shares a common base of knowledge. Although the nominating or board development committee is typically assigned responsibility to structure and oversee the process, the executive director should be an active participant and behind-the-scenes manager. This includes assembling the basic compilation of written material that is useful for board members to have in hand (bylaws, minutes of recent board meetings, board rosters, program and budget information); planning an event or other activity that brings board members in direct contact with the programs and services of the organization; and providing board members with meaningful ways to meet staff and volunteers. It may also mean time spent one-on-one with new members in order to learn more about them as well as letting them learn more about you.

MAKE THE MOST OF BOARD MEETINGS

Board meetings matter—to the organization, to the staff, to the executive director. It matters what boards do when they come together formally to work. It matters what they spend their time on, and how they deliberate. Meetings should not be perfunctory events, ritualized and empty of content, or worse, full of the wrong kind of content. Of all the areas where the executive director has the most direct influence and control over both the quality of the board's performance and the quality of the board/staff relationship, the board meeting is the most significant.

It is usually possible to map out most of a year's board meetings by looking at recurring events in the board's work: the budget approval process, the election of new members and officers, program or CEO evaluations, annual board retreats. This enables the director to budget his or her time and to keep staff notified of deadlines for the development of materials for board meetings. It also allows for an assessment of current meeting habits. Is the board meeting often enough? Too often? Are meetings too short? Interminable?

As was noted in an earlier chapter, the content of each meeting needs to be about things that matter to the organization and that, because of their strategic significance or consequence to the organization, legitimately qualify for the board's consideration. The director needs to help board members focus appropriately on agenda items and support their deliberations with information that provides insights into the issues under review.

When people praise a board they belong to, they are not just talking about the quality of the other board members, or the worthiness of the organization, or the brilliance and dedication of the staff. They are also talking about the sense of excitement and meaning they draw from their participation on the board. This sense of excitement and meaning should derive in substantial measure from the board meeting and the ease with which the work in that setting connects with the larger work of the organization. The structure and content of the board's meetings are too good an opportunity to build powerful relationships and maintain board effectiveness for an executive director to lose.

LEARN TO COMMUNICATE WITH THE BOARD

The one indisputable advantage the executive director will always have over the board is access to information. This is also the most valuable tool the executive director possesses to build an effective board. Insecure executive directors misuse this advantage to control and limit the board's engagement in issues. Between sharing too little and sharing too much, the director can leave a board either struggling to gain a foothold on a topic or swamped in a sea of facts and figures.

Sometimes the problem is not insecurity but a general inability on the part of an executive director to differentiate between information that tells a story and background noise. Information is useful only if it leads to insight and, ultimately, knowledge. For an executive director, this is a skill worth developing, and not just in relation to the board. It takes practice to master this skill. It is a minimalist's art to present only the information that is useful and to organize it in a legible form.

In addition to what to communicate, there is the equally important question of how often to communicate. The central communication event in the life of the organization is the board meeting, but executive directors are wise to think beyond and around this event. Board members will complain if they receive voluminous and frequent packets of information that take too much time to read. Too much paper usually becomes undifferentiated paper. This leaves board members in charge of deciding what's important and what can be ignored. This can seriously undermine a director's intentions, particularly if what is ignored are the background materials for the board meeting. The frequency and content of communication with the board will depend on the size and complexity of an organization's programs and the frequency of board meetings, but an executive director should think this through to make certain the organization is making the most of the board's time and attention.

At a different level, the executive director needs to have a more focused approach to direct communication with individual members of the board. It is important to stay in touch. Luckily, the phone and e-mail make informal but reassuring communications possible without unreasonable investments of time.

ENCOURAGE REFLECTION AND LEARNING

At regular intervals, the board needs opportunities to fine-tune its own work and learn something useful for its service to the organization. Reflection and learning are important tools for the board in its work. Although the executive director cannot force the board to be better, he or she can encourage this behavior and help to plan it.

Learning can be a way for the board to look outward from the organization to the wider world, helping board members to understand the pressures and influences that need to be acknowledged and understood if the organization is to remain relevant and vital. The executive director is more attuned to the environment in which the organization operates and can identify people and activities that can broaden the board's perspective. The commitment to learn continuously, and to place an organization's work in context, not only feeds the intellectual needs of the board, but also makes strategic thinking and decision making second nature to the board's point of view.

CONCLUSION

The natural tension that exists between the board and the executive director does not have to be the relationship's defining characteristic. An executive director is the principal beneficiary of a high-functioning board and fortunately has more resources and more opportunities to develop such a board than is often realized or used. The executive director beleaguered by an incompetent or inconsiderate board is a dated image. It might generate sympathy in some quarters, but soon becomes tiresome. Boards can be hard to work with, they can be difficult to engage in meaningful issues, and they can resist efforts to shift into a higher gear, but there is much that an executive director can do to change those behaviors. A good board is an asset to the organization and to the executive director and should be cultivated, just as any other asset would be.

CHAPTER 8

Saying Yes Twice: Engaging the Individual Board Member

I have a confession to make. A number of years ago I agreed to join the board of an organization in my community. Although this suburban community rivals a mid-size metropolitan area in terms of population, it is still remarkably small. People cross paths all the time, particularly if they have children. We meet in grocery stores, hardware stores, the library, the movie theater, the playing fields, all the places we go when not tied to our desks. I said yes to serving on this board because . . . well . . . because I was asked. I also liked the other people involved and I appreciated the work the organization did. I quickly realized that the board's meeting schedule was better than a fortuneteller in predicting my travel schedule. When I looked at the schedule of meetings, it was like looking into a crystal ball and seeing my days on the road, my nights in some hotel. I confess—I did not make a single meeting. That is not the worst part of the story. This is the worst part: I never called anyone to admit that I had made a terrible error and to offer to resign from the board. It doesn't matter that no one ever called me to find out where I was. I never called. I was a no-show. My punishment, in addition to an embarrassment that I will take to my grave, is that, years later, I still duck when I see any of my fellow board members. Believe me when I say this community is smaller than it looks.

Every parent uses a variation of the following admonishment: Do as I say, not as I do.

With my confession behind me and that instruction before us, the first commandment for all board members is: Resign from the board if it is not possible to do a good job. Pick up the phone and explain to the board chair why serving on the board is no longer an obligation you can meet, and don't be persuaded to change your mind if the chair attempts to dissuade you. Assume that she is just being polite and not conceding to a new low in expectations for individual board member performance.

The most assiduous efforts to shape a board and its work will fail if the individuals who serve on the board refuse to do their part. A better measure of an effective board than a strong committee structure or positive cash flow is the extent to which board members feel they are all equally engaged in the work of the board. Attendance may be a crude gauge of commitment, but it is still useful. It is as true in governance as it is in sports that half of winning is showing up.

WHAT IS THE JOB—EXACTLY?

A good board member says yes to board service at least twice. The first is to the invitation to serve; the second is to the work involved. It appears in an earlier chapter, but it is worth repeating: A board needs to define clearly what the minimum expectations are for successful service on the board. In addition, a board member needs some way to make the commitment to do the work explicit. Some boards have formal job descriptions that spell out what individuals are expected to do. The job description becomes the basis for extending the invitation to serve; it also becomes the basis for accepting the invitation. Such a document enables no one to be under any illusion about what board service entails. Other boards ask members to sign a yearly contract, making the agreement very specific and subject to renewal.

A contract for board service is not for every organization. To some board members, it may imply that without a signed document they couldn't be trusted to do what they agreed to do. Nevertheless, the psychological power of that concrete and public declaration is useful, and alternatives are worth exploring. These might include a yearly review of the current job description by the full board as a prelude to recruiting new board members, or making time to talk with each board member as his or her term comes up for renewal. After all, over a two- or three-year period, the needs of an organization can change, requiring changes at the board level. Not to mention that a member's availability or appetite for the work may also change. A formal review as a term ends gives a board member a chance to depart gracefully, with reputation intact.

When it is clear that a fair number of board members are not continuing to say yes with a glad heart, something more intensive may be required. For instance, the board chair in an organization struggling with a large board and very uneven participation among members had the full board do a self-assessment, asking each member to evaluate how the board as a whole performed in key respects. The chair then met individually with each member of the board to explore how the board's performance might be improved. Each interview served a dual purpose. It was an invitation to a member to contribute directly to making the board more effective and it was an opportunity for a member to signal a willingness to resign if service was no longer a good fit or a sufficiently high priority in the member's life. As time-consuming as the exercise was, it was a good investment for this particular organization and its board chair. Within a year, it had a smaller board, with highly engaged members and an invigorated fund-raising program. It is doubtful that this could have been achieved as quickly by any other means.

What does it take to be a successful member of a board? What does it take to enable each member to do his or her best? Despite some commonalities, there will be substantial variations among nonprofits. Starting a nonprofit requires a different set of skills and a different focus from the board than governing one with 50 years of experience. We need to appreciate those differences if boards are to work, not for some typical or theoretical organization, but for the organization that has decided it needs specific individuals to do specific work on its behalf. If board members are to be able to say yes to the work as well as the invitation, what exactly do they need to know as they consider the offer to join? Most boards need to be prepared to answer the following questions:

- What are the major issues the board is currently focused on?

- What talents, expertise, qualities, or characteristics is the board seeking in new members? What does the prospective candidate offer?

- How often does the board meet and, typically, for how long?

- Is everyone asked to serve on a committee? How are committee assignments made?

- What are the expectations for personal giving to the organization? Is there a minimum?

- What kind of fund raising is required of board members? Is there an annual campaign, a capital campaign in progress, or special events that require the financial support of the board?

- What is the relationship between the board and the executive director and between the board and other staff members?
- Is an orientation program in place? Are other board education activities offered?
- Does the board have an annual retreat of any kind?
- Are there changes on the horizon that a new board member should know about? The retirement of a long-time executive director, a major staff layoff, the prospect of legal action?

If the list appears long and a little downbeat, particularly at the end, it is more important to be clear and candid than to be brief and less than perfectly honest. In this respect, the list does not address one important issue: the character of the board and the quality of its work. With luck, the answer will brighten the conversation. Certainly, if it is a good board, do not hesitate to say so. If it is hard-working, make that clear. If it is going through a rough patch, admit it, but describe what is being done to change things for the better. This is first time the working culture of the board will be described to a new board member, and it may be this more than other things that will motivate a board member to step up to the work.

In addition to describing the work involved, always make it clear why a particular individual has been asked to join the board. It may be their head for business or their reputation in their chosen field, or it may be geography in combination with other necessary qualifications. Spell it out. If prospective board members have been invited to serve because of a characteristic they possess—their age, their gender, their race, their ethnicity, their wealth, their poverty—this should be stated up front. It is rare that a single characteristic is the only useful quality a potential board member possesses, so it should not be too hard to be completely honest about what the board wants to accomplish by inviting particular people into its work.

SAYING YES

With a clearer invitation and a more realistic understanding of what will be entailed, let's shift the focus to the board's newest member. How do you become a productive member of the board?

Make the Time

Being busy may be a game of one-upmanship elsewhere, but not on a board, where it must be taken for granted that everyone is equally busy but not too busy to be there. Assume that the people around the table have budgeted time in their busy schedules to be there because it is important to them. They have said yes to this obligation and probably no to others in order to be able to do this job well. There is little patience in a busy world for the person who has failed to make this calculation correctly.

Agree to serve on the board only if you have enough time to do it. Understand fully what the commitment involves, including meetings, volunteer activities, special events, committee assignments, orientation, and retreats. If during your tenure on the board, your ability to show up is compromised, offer to resign. People return to school, have children, need to care for aging parents, become ill, get new jobs. It is better to make an honorable exit than to hide behind the canned goods in the supermarket whenever you spy the board chair.

Having made time to do the job does not give the organization permission to waste it. If you look around and see that the board's time is not well spent—that meetings are too long or too frequent, that a more productive committee structure would streamline the board's work and reduce the time everyone spends on board work—it is important to raise the issue in a constructive way with the board chair and other board members. This may be the spur the board needs to rethink its habits and try a new approach. If it turns out that some on the board are in love with dysfunction and others are willing to tolerate it, it is probably not the board for you, however fine its mission and however willing you are to support it. Say goodbye with good grace and offer to be as helpful as possible in a different capacity.

Become a Learner

The smallest nonprofit organization is complex in ways not apparent to the casual observer, and, for the most part, a new board member is not much more than a casual observer for the first year on the board. It is important to become knowledgeable about the organization; not just to memorize and support the mission, but really to understand the work that takes place in the organization everyday, the people who are served, the things that are done well and the things that are neglected. Every organization has a history; it has faced a crisis or two; it has had a few lucky breaks. The way the organization operates today reflects all of that. The board also reflects the organization's history and, in its habits and idiosyncrasies, reflects the character of earlier boards or powerful board personalities. The sooner a new board member appreciates both the history of the organization and its current reality, the sooner he or she will be able to participate fully.

The obligation to be knowledgeable belongs to the individual board member. A good board and a smart executive director will design an orientation program that covers much of the required background material, but the individual board member must take this process and build on it. If some form of board member to board member mentoring system is not in place, create your own. Particularly before and after the first few board meetings, it is important to have someone who can help explain the agenda, provide a bit of history and background, give a few clues into the financial reports, and put the meeting in some perspective after it is over. This effort to put information and experience in context is not a thinly veiled excuse to gossip, but an intelligent effort to get at the full meaning of the board's work as well as its approach to work. For this reason, it is important to select as the source of this information and advice a board member who is both experienced and balanced. In some organizations, the executive director may play part of this role, but some caution is required when this occurs. A board member's authority is based in part on his objectivity. He can turn to the executive director for guidance, but should be careful to not to compromise his objectivity by appearing to be on the director's "side"—a partisan instead of a steward.

Prepare for board meetings. Keep track of background information. Board members have a deserved reputation as black holes for information. The staff beams material in their general direction and it is absorbed, never to emit any light or energy. Spend half an hour before a board meeting reading over the material that is sent in advance. If material is distributed at the meeting itself, ask for the time you need to read it through. Staff can spend a significant amount of time preparing for board and committee meetings. Reading the material is a minimum show of respect, not to mention the only way to know what is going on. If material comes too fast and furious to be absorbed, suggest a way to streamline communications rather than stop opening envelopes with the organization's return address.

Pay attention to deadlines. An executive director is rightly discouraged if board members fail to take the time to complete a performance evaluation or have to be reminded repeatedly before turning it in. It may be less personally unnerving but certainly just as professionally frustrating to have requests for reaction and comment also go unheeded.

Respect the Staff

There is a temptation among board members to underestimate the staff, and as a result either to redo the staff's work or to take it apart and leave it by the side of the road to be swept up later. This is an aspect of life in the nonprofit sector that makes executive directors wary and gives boards a bad name. The board can further handicap the relationship with the executive director by failing to see beyond the simple-minded responsibility to "hire and fire" to the real responsibility of the board, which is to hire the best person possible for the position and then to do everything in the board's power to make that person successful.

The board's relationship to the executive director is central and it will influence the quality of board service for good or ill. There may be a wealth of board interactions with other staff through committee work or special projects, but each must be carefully circumscribed by the primary obligation that board members have to the executive director, including the obligation not to undermine the proper working relationship between the director and his or her staff. Individual board members must resist the temptation to supervise the staff, to give them assignments, to discuss their performance with other board members, or to ask them to take any action that jeopardizes their relationship with the executive director.

There will be many instances when a board member has a more sophisticated grasp of certain activities, such as marketing or accounting, than either a small staff or a young staff may possess. There is a world of difference between offering those skills constructively to the staff and bludgeoning the staff with what you know and they don't. If you are concerned about the quality of staff work in a certain area, take it up quietly with the executive director first, before taking it up with the board chair or any other board member. Do not publicly feast on the staff's shortcomings, real or perceived.

If the organization has not attracted or managed to retain the staff it needs, it is a serious management issue, but one that the executive director should be expected to resolve and that the board should incorporate as part of the executive director's evaluation. In contrast, it might be also be a resource issue. There is a limit to the idea of doing more with less, despite the myth that prevails in the nonprofit sector. In this case the board has an obligation to look at the budget and program priorities to find a solution, commit to finding new resources, or accept reality.

See the Big Picture

The board needs to keep its eye firmly fixed on the big picture, and individual board members need to train themselves to do the same. It is human nature to start and stay with what we know, to focus on the doorbells of organizational life rather than venture into unfamiliar territory. Few people are gifted with the ability to see the big picture and think strategically. This is learned, not instinctive, behavior. Individual board members must practice, practice, practice if they hope to get good at it. Discipline yourself to stay out of the grass and keep your eye on the horizon. Linking the mission, the plan, the resources, and the results is a good way to begin to master a more strategic approach to the board's work. Temptation always lurks; when you look up at the ceiling and notice that a few lights are burned out, don't look down at the budget and ask how much has been budgeted for light bulbs this year.

Individual board members need to commit to keeping the board's focus on what matters. This means both self-discipline and a little constructive coaching for others on the board. If time in meetings is not well budgeted, suggest to the chair and the executive director ways to organize the agenda that might allow more time for important issues as well as things that might improve the level or the focus of the discussions. Learn the magic words and practice them before each meeting: "I think this is something we should let the staff decide. It is really an administrative decision. I don't think we should be spending time on it."

Have Courage

Boards are often called upon to make difficult decisions. In a health clinic that served an extremely poor population, the board chair described courage as the first responsibility of individual board members. It was the courage to make tough choices about allocating scarce resources, and the courage to defend those choices to the community. While it may provide a momentary surge of self-righteousness to let people know that you stood against a decision in the face of overwhelming odds, it is not a credit to you to be perceived by your peers as unreliable and by the organization's constituency as essentially powerless. It is more courageous to leave a board and work for change in a different manner than to undermine the efforts of the board to do what it believes to be the right thing.

It takes a different kind of courage to maintain a productive working culture for the board. It requires the courage to challenge peers periodically to remember why they are on the board. Every board member must contribute to good working relationships and act to protect them when they are threatened. It makes no sense to be victimized by unruly or unproductive behavior, particularly as a volunteer, or to watch an organization suffer because the board is trapped in conflict. It is extremely frustrating to believe in the mission of the organization and be willing to commit your time and energy to it and have that belief and commitment wasted. Rather than head

133

for the hills, make an effort to put unproductive behavior in its place by pointing out your lack of support for it and your concerns about what it is costing the organization in time, board involvement, and staff morale. Why give the least useful member or members of the board the greatest power to shape the work of the board and the future of the organization?

Keep Issues on the Table Not under It

There should be no hidden agendas in the boardroom or among board members, no cabals, no star chambers. Keep the board's work in the boardroom where everyone who has agreed to serve should have equal access to information and an equal opportunity to wield authority and make decisions. Everyone who serves on a board has taken on an identical set of responsibilities and legal obligations. Everyone has sacrificed his or her time to support the mission of the organization. Despite the disparity that may exist among board members as donors to the organization, the largest contribution does not confer the right to have one's way. In the same way, tenure on the board or status as the founder does not grant automatic rights of refusal. Deference to experience or gratitude for service rendered is not permission to dictate the board's actions.

Be Prepared to Lead

Not everyone is cut out to be the chair of the board, but if there is a potential match between talent, temperament, and time, do not resist the invitation to take on a leadership role. It is hard to be the chair, but it is even harder to serve on a board that lacks good leadership. Practice assuming leadership by meeting other shorter-term obligations on the board in a responsible manner. Make it a point to model good board behavior. Avoid false modesty.

Say Thank You and Goodbye

A little turnover is a beautiful thing. A board needs to remain a dynamic asset in the life of the organization. It cannot do that if the composition and membership of the board are static. People can learn new tricks, but new people come with new tricks ready-made.

It may be flattering to be seen as irreplaceable, but it is not really a compliment when on a board. It can signal laziness on the part of the nominating committee more than admiration. Who wants to be the bird in the hand?

If you have been a good board member and created value for the organization, you have done your part. You might be enticed to return after a bit of a vacation, but such invitations should be carefully weighed. It is a big world, filled with interesting and talented people; an organization needs to engage as many of those people as possible and will never succeed if it goes only with what it knows and loves. As a good steward and a friend of the organization, challenge it to renew the board at every opportunity.

CHAPTER 9

Fine-Tuning the Instrument

An earlier chapter drew a comparison between a board and an orchestra. To be of any value, each in their different ways must work together; they need good leadership; and they definitely need to practice. However, unlike musicians, board members do not bring years of training to their performances. They rarely study for their role, and their practice time is sharply limited. Board members typically learn nonprofit governance incrementally, a meeting at a time. Some have the benefit of educational activities geared to their needs, but at the best of times these efforts can be irregular and sometimes haphazard. Basically, board members are expected to hammer out a tune within moments of entering the boardroom—ready or not. Even with these disadvantages, many boards manage to do extremely well. Those that prosper against the odds are those that take responsibility for the quality of their performance, rather than leaving it to chance, and create a culture in which the idea of continuous improvement is paid more than lip service. They understand the value of what they do in the organization, and take their role seriously. The quality of their work is important to them because it is important to the organizations they serve.

There are numerous incidental moments when a board and its members have a shot at self-improvement: when a board meeting begins to break down and board members themselves bring it back on track; when a board realizes it doesn't know enough to make a good decision and sets out to get better prepared; when a committee develops a plan of action that everyone on it agrees to honor. A board that is even a little self-conscious about its role will automatically take the opportunities that routine board work provides to be more effective. They do all add up. Nevertheless, there are a handful of moments in the cycle of a board's work when, with a little planning, the time, talent, and receptivity of the group can be leveraged to exceptionally good effect.

These moments can be approached sequentially or as close to simultaneously as the board can manage. Because they occur naturally in the life of a board and happen with some regularity, they provide a particularly strong foundation for both incidental opportunities for improvement and more carefully planned board development activities. These basic activities are the identification and cultivation of new members, the board's orientation program, and the regular self-assessment a board undertakes of its role and its performance. Each in its way constitutes a perfect moment for a board tune-up, because they are all integral, almost unavoidable, parts of a board's working agenda. Finding new members is something that most boards do annually. Orienting new people to board service might not occur with the same highly desirable regularity as the election of new members; nevertheless, it has a logic that even the busiest board with the busiest members would find hard to resist. Finally, a board self-assessment is a glorified way to describe the formal self-scrutiny that should precede asking anyone new to join a board—a bit of best foot forward.

IDENTIFYING NEW MEMBERS

The most important committee of the board is the nominating committee. No other committee has such direct responsibility for the quality of the board. Despite its importance, it has also become one of the least attractive board assignments. The nominating committee has very hard work to do and the quality of its work can't be hidden or disguised. Leave the work until the last minute, and the chances of recruiting a full slate of new board members before the election become very slim—and the recruitment tactics can become quite desperate. This desperation fueled by a looming deadline may be the source of the big lie with which so many members have been enticed to mediocre board performance: Please say yes. It won't take much time.

One reason for the anxious air that hangs about nominating committees is the timing of their formation and the schedule of their work. It is not enough to form the committee weeks before the election or for a committee that has been standing for a year to begin its work moments before it has to. The nominating committee is a genuine standing committee of the board, one with work to do on a year-round basis. Its basic charge is both simple and formidable: to build the best board possible by recruiting the best people to the task. It is responsible for the quality of the board's composition and responsible for the quality of board members' individual performance. This is the committee's assignment and meeting it should bring out the best in committee members. Sometimes the charge is expanded to include the quality of the board's performance overall. When the committee is given this larger responsibility, it is often renamed something that reflects the scope of that charge, such as the board development committee or the committee on trusteeship.

It is not the nominating committee's job to find new board members. It is the committee's job to manage the process on behalf of the board. This may seem like splitting hairs, but it is an important distinction. The board should not say to the committee, "Go out and find us a few good members." It should more correctly say, "Help us find a few good members." Finding the right combination of skill and dedication for the board's work is the responsibility of the full board. It should engage everyone on the board at different points throughout the year, from spelling out the ground rules and the rationale for joining the board (otherwise known as a job description) to keeping ears and eyes open for potential candidates. The process should also engage the executive director and, to a lesser extent, the staff. It can be very challenging for board members alone to search wide enough for the kinds of candidates who are needed. The staff are often more alert to the possibilities. The nominating committee serves as the gathering point for the ideas and suggestions that emerge and helps to organize a process that makes good recruitment possible.

The nominating committee requires two critical pieces of intelligence to do its job. The first is a working definition of what it takes to be a successful member of the board; the second is a fairly precise description of the kind of person the board needs and the committee is searching for.

Developing a job description is a collective exercise that should engage the full board well before the first new person is approached for board service. It evolves from three very simple but important questions: What are the major issues that face the organization in the next two or three years? What does that mean for the board's work? What will it take for board members to be successful in accomplishing these tasks?

One board confronted these questions after having weathered a complex interval when the board's stability needed to counter the turbulence of the organization's daily existence. Faced with an increasingly erratic performance from a long-standing executive director, a capital campaign in disarray, and financial problems that threatened to bring activities to a halt, the board deliberately opted to stay small and retain key members without regard to term limits. Three or four board members, pushed by a very powerful and focused chair, provided intense leadership to the organization and support for the new executive director. They could trust each other to do the right thing without too much discussion or dissent, and capitalized on those assets to keep the organization on the move. After a few years of this, the chair and the executive director took a deep breath, looked up, and decided the worst was over; now the biggest threat to the organization was the narrow base of its leadership. The enterprise depended on too few people to get things done and couldn't continue in that way for too much longer. As gratifying as it had been to play the role of saviors so successfully, the board recognized the need to broaden both participation and support, so it began a three-year program of board recruitment. They did this by first deciding what needed to be done, then looking carefully for the best people around. They gave themselves three years in which to accomplish their plan in order to balance the need for new talent and energy with the equally important need to maintain the board's efficiency as it doubled in size.

It is worth noting that this board violated a number of items of common wisdom about good governance. A very small group maintained tight control. Term limits were suspended and were never reactivated even after the board began to grow in size. They took three years to complete the increase in size. And, they left to last the issue of succession for the board chair. Nevertheless, it was an extremely effective board in spite of its unorthodoxy. They understood what needed to happen, worked only with the best interests of the organization in mind, valued results over process, and were quick to discipline board members who fiddled with management issues or broke ranks to work on personal agendas. Their strongest asset through the transition they were carefully managing was the clarity of their plan to reshape the board.

The concept of a recruitment plan is a useful one. A board doesn't come together for a year, stop, and begin again. The board's role is continuous and evolving. It has a responsibility to sustain itself and to do this it must be able both to fill immediate gaps in its membership and to anticipate what will be needed. In a national survey of board practice, the average length of service for board members was six years, typically broken into terms of either two or three years.* The good news about terms of office is that continuity and sustainability can easily be managed when board members are serving for predictable periods of time. The need for change while maintaining continuity can also be accommodated without too much additional effort. The bad news is that three years, never mind six years, is a long time to live with mistakes. The maxim about repenting at leisure takes on new meaning when hasty actions are immortalized at the board level.

A plan is easy to develop and there are many resources available to help standardize the process. The first step in building a recruitment plan is to think carefully about the first two questions listed earlier: What issues will have to be addressed in the next three to five years? What does that mean for the board's work? The nominating committee may be able to answer those questions in a preliminary way before taking its conclusions to the board, but the full board is just as good a place to have the preliminary discussion. It is a matter of deciding which group makes the best editor of the working draft, the committee or the board.

With an agreement about what is facing the organization and what it will take for the board to do its part, the nominating committee can create a picture of the ideal board. Does the organization need to extend its reach geographically? What does that mean in terms of the networks or relationships that board members can bring to this issue? Is it important that the organization strengthen its access to policy makers? What kinds of experience or background would make a board mem-

---

*A Snapshot of America's Nonprofit Boards, National Center for Nonprofit Boards, 1997.

ber effective in this arena? Are we mounting a capital campaign? Do we need to find someone who has successfully planned or led such a campaign in the last couple of years?

The ideal board is a mix of characteristics, skills, and experiences. The ideal mix is dictated not by a formula or by admiration of another organization's board; it is dictated by what the specific, individual organization requires. The characteristics will include things that have unique functional value to the organization as well as symbolic value. The required characteristics may involve gender, age, race, ethnicity, geographical location, or consumer experience. The list of characteristics must be driven by each organization. In some organizations it will be important that a board member's title on the job always be chief executive; in others, it will be important that rural and urban experiences be included at the board level.

Skills are generally easier to itemize. Again, the goal is to have a board that reflects what the organization needs. If you don't need the board to provide legal counsel and advice, there is no need to place a premium on identifying attorneys solely for their professional qualifications. At the end of the day, the nominating committee may recruit a number of lawyers to the board, but it will be for other reasons.

Experience and skills overlap in many cases, but it is still worth distinguishing between the two in building the ideal board. It may be equally important to have members who have been actively engaged in specific kinds of fund raising and those who through their work or civic life, have strong networks and affiliations that can be put to good use. If the two attributes can be found in one person—great, but it is important to acknowledge the need for both and not assume they will be found together.

With the ideal board mapped out, reality then comes into play. How many of the current board members fill the requirements identified in the map of the ideal board? Are there members who will retire from the board in the next two years and take with them significant characteristics, skills, or experience? In comparing the current board to the ideal board, it is important to look beyond the characteristics, skills, and experience that a particular board member represents and consider how well a member has made those qualities available to the organization. A board member from a particular part of the state has not provided the board with the geographic representation and credibility it hoped to have if he or she rarely makes it to board meetings.

At the conclusion of this step, gaps will be evident. These should be assigned priorities—which characteristics are most important, what skill set is the most highly desirable, what kinds of experience does the organization most urgently need to tap? A recruitment plan extends beyond the current year election deadline to a period two to three years out. It ranks the board's needs so that board members and staff can be alert for board talent but focused on a few immediate requirements. Everyone in the organization must be familiar with the plan, because everyone in the organization is involved in generating suggestions—suggestions, not invitations—for the nominating committee. The nominating committee manages the recruitment process, making sure it is orderly and reflects the seriousness of purpose at its heart.

The final element in the preliminary phase of the nominating committee's work is the answer to a third question: What does it take to be a successful member of the board? The job description must be in place before any potential member can be approached about his or her interest in the position.

A tough assignment for the nominating committee, but one it needs to embrace, is the assessment of board members whose terms are up for renewal. One of the virtues of taking care with each of the preliminary steps required to recruit the right people for the right job is that it rationalizes the need to assess current members for their ability to continue to add value to the board. It should not take a full board term for a member's lack of responsibility to be addressed; a good chair deals with problems such as attendance and poor performance when they occur, not waiting two or three years for the nominating committee to do the dirty work. Still, the conclusion of a term is an appropriate place to evaluate a more subtle range of problems. Is a board member chronically unhappy or out of step with decision making? Are the member's motives for board service too mixed to be ignored? Has the organization grown more complex and the requirements to be an effective steward grown more complex with it? There are many reasons why a board member may no longer be a good fit or a happy fit with the organization. The renewal of a term is a natural and welcome moment to test for appropriateness as well as for a willingness to renew the commitment it takes to continue successfully.

Nominating committees flounder and boards find themselves ignoring term limits because of the difficulty of finding people to recruit. A large part of the difficulty can be traced to lack of good preparation and to depending on too few people to do the job. Two or three people are quickly going to run out of friends and colleagues, and burn through their Rolodexes. Boards can also be too insular and unable to cast a wide net even when the full board is invited to participate. This is a reason to consider drawing non-board members into the process, perhaps as members of the nominating committee.

A board that is ineffective and knows it, or is filled with members who are bored and unhappy with their role, is not going to be vigorous in its recruitment of new members. Failure in these cases is a self-fulfilling prophecy. Better to focus on getting better as a board, or recruiting only a few people with that clear assignment in mind than to invite able people to join a lackluster group and then watch them fall away as the truth is revealed. Even the promise of a board assignment that will take no time and require no fund raising will not compensate for a thoroughly tedious experience.

One interesting aberration to note in connection with the challenge of finding good prospective candidates is the rejection out of hand of anyone who steps up and volunteers to serve on the board. A public appetite for the job appears unseemly and is a little unsettling. A board could be on life support and still find a way to say no to someone who expresses an open interest in serving on the board, even if he or she appears to be highly qualified. Nonprofits require that board members be courted and invited; boards prefer to choose rather than acquiesce. This is why few organizations outside of associations and membership groups advertise their search for board members as they would a staff vacancy, instead relying on a system that combines the maximum effort to cull prospects with the minimum exposure to unwanted attention.

ORIENTATION

Orientation is a way to make people feel both welcome and smart. It should begin well before a board member is elected, while the investigation and cultivation phase is underway. Good people will not be persuaded by written material alone to say yes to board service, and everyone should be wary of garnering a commitment just on the basis of a few current board members' ability to charm a prospective candidate over lunch or during a meeting. Board members cannot know the organization only through the prism of board service. It is important to get close to the ground periodically and watch the organization in action before joining the board and to do it again very systematically shortly thereafter.

Orientation is a not a single event; it is a process. We should assume that it will take a full year for a board member to grasp the detail as well as see the underlying depth of the organization's life and the board's work. Although a large concentrated period of learning can be organized shortly after the election to board service or prior to the first meeting, a little planning will enable a much broader and well-focused orientation process to be developed. For instance, one organization invited board candidates to attend the planning retreat that was scheduled to take place a few months before their election. The material prepared in advance of the retreat and the discussions that took place during the retreat were a powerful way for incoming board members to learn the context for their work for the next two to three years. Another board gave incoming members the dates of significant organizational events taking place within the first six months of their terms, both to make sure the dates got onto their calendars and to help them understand how helpful their attendance would be in getting familiar with the organization.

Building the social interaction among board members is also a critical part of building board effectiveness, and the orientation of new members should include explicit opportunities for new board members to meet and learn about their new peers from a personal perspective. The reverse is also true. The sooner long-term members come to know new members, the sooner the team can expand to incorporate and use the new talent in the room. As busy as people are, they are still willing to give an evening, a long lunch, or a breakfast to the goal of making people feel welcome.

BOARD SELF-ASSESSMENT

How good are we as a board? A board must become the best judge of that if its judgments are to have any power to influence either the work that is done or the ways in which that work is approached. Like other kinds of evaluation, board members are making judgments and assessments of the board and each other all the time. Unfortunately, the natural tendency to exercise our critical faculties and form opinions is useful to a board only if it is organized. Even if it is perversely satisfying, there is no value in conducting evaluations in the parking lot or on the phone the day after a meeting.

A board self-assessment can take many forms and a number of resources are available to help a board undertake the process. The bibliography includes a number of sources for off-the-shelf products. When shopping for such a product, avoid anything that can't be easily adapted. Typically, boards are asked to complete a standard questionnaire that may or may not coincide with the responsibilities and concerns they actually have. If there is a mismatch between the questionnaire and the board's sense of itself, it can affect how thoughtfully the board completes it. The process for collating or reporting results may also be unnecessarily complex or time-consuming, raising an additional obstacle to using the results in a constructive way. If a standardized process is used, it is important that the questionnaire be easy to tailor and that the results be easy to read and interpret. Most board members are not mathematicians or social scientists; they are reading the results for the big picture they paint of the board's strengths and weaknesses in order to address the best ways to improve.

Finding an appropriate evaluation instrument is not the biggest hurdle to self-assessment; the biggest hurdle is finding the time and dedication to do it. To succeed, a self-assessment requires the following:

- A commitment from the full board to participate
- A committee or small group with the assignment to oversee the process and manage the results
- A clear timetable that covers when the self-assessment questionnaire will be distributed, when it will be returned, and when it will be reviewed by the full board
- Time set aside during a regular board meeting or for a special meeting to review the results

- An action plan that addresses the weaknesses the board perceives in its role or structure
- A way to monitor whether the action plan is being realized.

The elements covered in a self-assessment are more important than the process, but a poorly designed process or one without the support and confidence of the board will never succeed no matter how well-conceived the focus of the instrument.

A board need not use an off-the-shelf product; it can create its own questionnaire. This requires more time on the part of one or two board members, but it also results in a more targeted process. A sample range of issues and questions might cover:

- Mission: Is the mission used to make decisions? Is it current?
- Board composition and structure: Is the talent the organization needs represented on the board? Does the committee structure function?
- Board meetings: Do meetings focus on the right issues? Does the board have the information it needs to make decisions? Is there adequate time for discussion and debate?
- Board/Staff relations: Does the board respect the authority of the executive director? Is the evaluation of the executive director useful to the board and to the director?
- Programs: Does the board evaluate programs for their effectiveness?
- Finances: Does the board understand the budget process? Does it read and understand the financial reports?
- Fund raising: Does the board understand the plan for resource development? Does the board understand its obligations to help raise funds?

For ease of scoring, board members need a simple mechanism for indicating whether they feel they are doing a good

149

job or not. However, a simple checklist deprives board members of the opportunity to be reflective. It is important to ask board members not just how they feel, but how they would propose to make things better. This open-ended question provides a rich source of information and ideas to the board. It is such a significant resource that when the results are collated, it is important to share as many of the responses with the full board as possible.

For most boards, attempting a broad self-assessment on an annual basis would be self-defeating. There is a limit to how much new information will be generated in a year. A thorough self-assessment can probably be done every other year or every third year. It is a critical step if the board is about to undertake a major reorganization. It is also a particularly useful way to build a foundation for organizational planning. The critical thinking and reflection that the self-assessment generates create a positive frame of mind for planning and serve to motivate the board.

If a full self-assessment can't be done, for whatever reason, it is still helpful for the board to look at a single issue or a group of board functions and organize a way to get feedback from its members. It is critical that boards find ways to assess themselves. The habit matters almost as much as the outcome, although the outcome is almost always valuable. Boards are expected to engage in a wide variety of evaluation activities as part of their responsibilities to the organization: financial evaluation, program evaluation, and the evaluation of the executive director. A regular process of self-evaluation makes the board a little more humble about evaluation, a little less likely to see itself as "in charge" and free of blame when people and programs come before it for review. A board that wants to be good at what it does will move beyond the incidental opportunities it has to improve performance and approach the improvement of its own capacity systematically.

CONCLUSION

When a board views itself as an asset to the organization, it is prepared to see its effectiveness as a strategic advantage. In this light, a range of activities that might appear to some to be glorified housekeeping can be pursued with energy and rigor because of their ability to enhance and strengthen an important organizational asset. Activities such as identification and cultivation of new members and board orientation are seen properly to be cornerstones of a board's capacity. Developing a job description for the board and minimum expectations for individual performance move from being pro forma activities to become fundamental agreements among board members about purpose and performance.

A focus on the board's underlying value to the organization provides clarity to the board's work and a framework for measuring success. With this focus, it is possible to look critically at board function, board composition, the information and educational needs of the board, and the best structure for the board's work, and make the investments necessary to enhance performance.

CHAPTER 10

Closing Thoughts

Dr. Spock began his famous baby book by directing these words to parents: "You know more than you realize." Without pushing the parallels too far, boards also know more than they realize. Boards have few illusions. They know when they are working well and they know when something is wrong. Given a reason to be better and some guidance and support along the way, a board can change itself and change the way in which it is valued in the organization. It helps that board members bring good will to the assignment; it helps that board service is a volunteer activity and not the byproduct of pressure or coercion; it helps that board members are people who have been asked to be there, usually for a good reason. These are excellent raw materials for strengthening the performance of the board.

Boards can be similar in their excellence and different in their approaches to achieving it. This is an important distinction. Each board must fit its performance to the needs of the organization it serves and be willing to change as the organization changes. A million nonprofits will arrive at almost as many variations in strategies for achieving good governance. The only criterion that matters is whether the organization is better because of the board's efforts on its behalf.

This willingness to abandon prescriptions in favor of what is in the best interests of the organization demands a level of reflection and open-mindedness that is within the reach of every board. Success is enhanced by patience on the part of individual board members, thoughtful leadership on the part of the board chair, and the confidence and support of the executive director.

When boards fail to be effective, or as effective as they could be, the problems can usually be traced to an underestimation of the potential benefit of a strong board rather than a willful effort to incapacitate it. Of course, there are exceptions. Board members can cast themselves as innocent bystanders holding everyone and everything but themselves responsible for wobbly performance—a weak chair, incompetent colleagues, an executive director in over her head. A board can be handicapped by an executive director who is happy with a weak board or a founder who wants acolytes rather than peers. It may be suffering from the cumulative effect of years of confusion and bad habits. All of these conditions can be remedied. Granted, it can be an uphill struggle, but if these obstacles can be resolved the results will make the efforts worthwhile.

Cyril Houle in *Governing Boards: Their Nature and Nurture* wrote "a good board is a victory, not a gift."

Often all it takes to make a board work is one or two board members who strike a responsive note with their peers or with a frustrated executive director. The board has it within its power to change the status quo by first demanding more of itself and its members, and renegotiating its relationship with the executive director and other members of the staff. The encouraging part of this process is the disproportionate results to be achieved with relatively small investments.

A board that works is an enticing prospect and one well within reach.

You know more than you realize.

Begin.

Resources

Over the years, I have found the following publications to be useful and accessible, often stimulating.

GOVERNANCE AND BOARD DEVELOPMENT

Nonprofit Board Answer Book, Robert C. Andringa and Ted W. Engstrom. National Center for Nonprofit Boards, 1998.

Most of the questions are basic and most of the answers are practical. An easy way to check to see what two sensible, experienced practitioners have to say on a subject.

Governing Boards, Cyril O. Houle. Jossey-Bass and the National Center for Nonprofit Boards, 1989.

A comprehensive, somewhat stately, book that covers all aspects of effective governance.

The Effective Board of Trustees, Richard P. Chait, Thomas P. Holland, and Barbara E. Taylor. American Council on Education, 1991.

Improving the Performance of Governing Boards, Richard P. Chait, Thomas P. Holland, and Barbara E. Taylor. American Council on Education, 1996.

Two of the most thoughtful and thought provoking books to be published on governance. Although the first book focuses on boards in higher education, it identifies a set of characteristics common to effective boards that is widely applicable. The second book looks at the best ways to shift the focus of a board's work to issues of strategic value.

Boards that Make a Difference: A New Design for Leadership in Non-profit and Public Organizations, John Carver. Jossey-Bass, 1990.

This book introduced the Policy Governance model and struck a chord in the nonprofit sector. The model has the value of rigor and prompted many boards to re-organize their thinking. The model is challenging to think about, but, to my mind, rigid and a little too arid when implemented to be a good fit for many organizations.

The Board Member's Book: Making a Difference in Voluntary Organizations, Brian O'Connell. Independent Sector, 1994.

A comprehensive and positive book that provides both the context for good governance and the elements of successful trusteeship.

Guidebook for Directors of Nonprofit Corporations. American Bar Association, 1993.

A clear and authoritative guide to the legal principles that apply to boards and the issues to which boards need to be attentive to feel confident they are playing by the rules.

MEETINGS AND COMMITTEES

10 Minutes to Better Board Meetings, Norah Holmgren. Planned Parenthood Federation, 1997.

A terrific, well-organized and sensible guide to better meetings, although what 10 minutes has to do with it is a mystery.

Robert's Rules of Order. Scott, Foresman, 1982.

The guide to every imaginable event that can occur in a meeting and how to resolve it.

Nonprofit Board Committees: How to Make Them Work, Ellen Cochran Hirzy. National Center for Nonprofit Boards, 1993.

The booklet describes the basic committees, their charges and how to make them worth having at all.

The Nominating Committee: Laying a Foundation for Your Organization's Future, Ellen Cochran Hirzy. National Center for Nonprofit Boards, 1994.

The title says it all.

EVALUATION AND ASSESSMENT

Assessment of the Chief Executive: A Tool for Boards and Chief Executives of Nonprofit Organizations, Jane Pierson and Joshua Mintz. National Center for Nonprofit Boards, 1995.

This is a comprehensive tool, even if a little unwieldy. It has the advantage of being published with a computer disk, which allows the tool to be tailored to be of maximum use to board and executive director.

Self-Assessment for Nonprofit Governing Boards, Larry H. Slesinger. National Center for Nonprofit Boards, rev. 1995.

This process uses the basic responsibilities of the board as the framework for the evaluation. Each section includes the open-ended question: How can the board do better? An individual self-evaluation is included.

Measuring Board Effectiveness: A Tool for Strengthening Your Board, Thomas P. Holland and Myra Blackmon. National Center for Nonprofit Boards, 2000.

This self-assessment process uses six key board competencies as the framework. These derive from research and writing by Holland on the boards of higher education organizations. The questions throughout the self-assessment are thought-provoking.

Board Assessment of the Organization, Peter Szanton. National Center for Nonprofit Boards, 1992.

A brief but extremely useful overview of the board's role in evaluating an organization's performance, including a handful of pointed questions that serve as a basic framework for this type of evaluation.

BOARD CULTURE

Keeping the Peace: Resolving Conflict in the Boardroom, Marion Peters Angelica. National Center for Nonprofit Boards, 2000.

Touches all the bases and combines common sense with a finely nuanced sense of what's really at work when conflict appears in the boardroom.

FINANCIAL STEWARDSHIP

Understanding Nonprofit Financial Statements: A Primer for Board Members, John Paul Dalsimer, 1995.

This is probably as much as a non-accountant board member wants to read on the subject and even it may be too much. A book is not the best tool for learning this basic and important subject.

STRATEGIC PLANNING

Strategic Planning Workbook for Nonprofits, Bryan Barry. Amherst H. Wilder Foundation, 1986.

Strategic Planning for Nonprofit Organizations: A Practical Guide and Workbook, Michael Allison and Jude Kaye, John Wiley & Sons, Inc., 1997.

Both good, basic books on the subject. Well-organized, easy to follow, light on jargon.

FUND RAISING

Speaking of Money: A Guide to Fund Raising for Nonprofit Board Members, video. National Center for Nonprofit Boards, 1996.

A great overview of the board's role in fund raising. It touches on the personal difficulties and fears board members have with fund raising, as well as the satisfaction that comes with doing it successfully.

Index